Scalawags

Other books by Jim Christy

*The Price of Power*
(a biography of Charles Bedaux)

*Flesh and Blood*
(a study of professional boxing)

*The Redemption of Anna Dupree* (novel)

*Nine O'clock Gun* (novel)

*Tight Like That* (stories)

*Cavatinas* (poetry)

Also, recently released:
*God's Little Angle*
(a CD of poetry and songs)

# SCALAWAGS

Rogues, Roustabouts, Wags &
Scamps—Brazen Ne'er-Do-Wells
Through the Ages

by Jim Christy

Copyright © 2008 by Jim Christy

Anvil Press Inc.
P.O. Box 3008, Main Post Office
Vancouver, BC V6B 3X5 CANADA
www.anvilpress.com

First Printing.

All rights reserved. No part of this book may be reproduced by any means without the prior written permission of the publisher, with the exception of brief passages in reviews. Any request for photocopying or other reprographic copying of any part of this book must be directed in writing to ACCESS: The Canadian Copyright Licensing Agency, One Yonge Street, Suite 800, Toronto, Ontario, Canada, M5E 1E5

LIBRARY AND ARCHIVES CANADA CATALOGUING IN PUBLICATION

Christy, Jim, 1945-
   Scalawags : rogues, roustabouts, wags & scamps : brazen ne'er-do-wells through the ages / Jim Christy.

ISBN: 978-1-895636-94-9

1. Rogues and vagabonds—Biography. 2. Rogues and vagabonds—History. I. Title.

CT9980.C47 2008    364.1092'2    C2008-904948-9

Printed and bound in Canada
Cover design: Derek von Essen
Interior design & typesetting: HeimatHouse
Author photo: Virginia Lawson

Represented in Canada by the Literary Press Group
Distributed by the University of Toronto Press

   The publisher gratefully acknowledges the financial assistance of the Canada Council for the Arts, the Book Publishing Industry Development Program (BPIDP) and the Province of British Columbia through the BC Arts Council and the Book Publishing Tax Credit.

# DEDICATION

To those with Scalawagish tendencies, wherever they may be.

And especially to the memory of Count Telfrin, AKA Russian Jack Tattenbaum, a member of the Clanton Gang, whose leader was my great-great grandfather, Newman Clanton. Russian Jack's former gang was that of the Czar's Imperial White Hussars. Given his penchant for delivering Shakespeare from the stage of the Bird Cage in Tombstone, Arizona, it is thus appropriate that he met his end at Shakespeare, New Mexico Territory, where he was hanged for horse stealing in 1883. It turned out that all his wild stories, that few believed, were true after all. Which goes to show you never can tell.

ACKNOWLEDGEMENTS

The idea for the "Scalawags" column originated in the active imagination of former *NUVO* Managing Editor Lyndon Grove, who didn't know me from Slim Gaillard but took the chance at the prompting of the late and much lamented Phil Surguy.

To expand the piece on Tillson Lever Harrison from the version originally published in *NUVO Magazine*, I consulted the article "'I dare do all . . .': The saga of Dr. Tillson Lever Harrison" by Allan E. Levine, published in the *Canadian Medical Association Journal* (November 6, 2007).

# Table of Malcontents

*Foreword* Cameron Johnson | 9
*Introduction* Jim Christy | 11

## The Scalawags

Tallulah Bankhead | 15
William Beckford | 20
John Romulus Brinkley | 26
Ned Buntline | 31
Lord Buckley | 38
Count di Cagliostro | 43
Marchesa Luisa Casati | 49
Samuel Franklin Cody | 54
Morris "Two-Gun" Cohen | 60
Arthur Cravan | 65
Charles Cros | 71
Lady Jane Digby | 76
Florence Lowe "Pancho" Barnes | 81
Elsa von Freytag Loringhoven | 86
Slim Gaillard | 92
Tillson Lever Harrison | 97
Sadakichi Hartmann | 105
Al Jennings | 110
Alfred "Lash" LaRue | 115
Trebitsch Lincoln | 120
Eliza Lynch | 125

Adah Menken | 130

Count Geoffrey Potocki de Montalk | 136

Lola Montez | 142

Comte de Waldeck | 148

Bernarr Macfadden | 153

Wilson Mizner | 159

Count Navratillini | 166

Kiki of Montparnasse | 172

Louis De Rougemont | 177

Harriette Wilson | 182

William Seabrook | 187

Titanic Thompson | 192

George Francis Train | 198

Alma Werfel | 204

Jack Purvis | 210

*Index* | 217

*Author Biographical Note* | 224

# Foreword

The best description I can make of Jim Christy's "Scalawags" column is to compare his writings to a particularly well-aged scotch. Each story focuses on the adventures of one particular rogue or another, to the effect that they are not unlike a shelf of expensive bottles: they're all rich and wealthy of character, they're invariably unique, and they are an absolute pleasure to taste. And just as an expensive scotch is something to savour on special occasions, in the case of "Scalawags", which has appeared in every issue of NUVO magazine since 2000, it's been a treat that comes around four times a year.

NUVO is a quarterly, and the schedule of a magazine that's published every three months is a mixed blessing. On one hand, those ridiculous deadlines that lead to early-onset insanity in the editors of dailies, weeklies and monthlies only come once a season. On the other hand, when those deadlines do arrive, they are intense, a barely navigable maelstrom of edits and proofs and corrections.

But one thing that provides some measure of respite amongst the regular craziness is the *Scalawags* column. And when that e-mail from Jim comes in, no matter where I am—on the road or sitting in my office—I make time to read about whatever incredible personality he's chosen this time. It's consistently entertaining, and it's not just the staff at the magazine who think so; it's a favourite of our readers, and we frequently get feedback to that extent.

Jim's been writing the column for almost a decade. That's made for a lot of scalawags. Part of me has always wondered if Jim would ever run out of subjects, and have to stop painting these fascinating historical portraits. It hasn't happened yet, and I'm not too worried. Jim has a knack for searching out a good story, and I'm sure there are myriad more to tell.

For that, indeed, is Jim's gift. Writing is his craft, and he has an incredible talent for finding, and telling, a tale. Like all the great storytellers, his witty and measured delivery keeps you interested and—in the case of us at *NUVO*—eagerly awaiting the next story.

Ultimately, it is the lives of the subjects—sometimes tragic, always odd, and frequently hilarious—that stay with us, long after reading. Given the prodigious experiences these characters have had, one can only hope that they—and their stories—will remain immortal.

And they surely will, if Jim has anything to say about it. Which he does.

After reading about a few of the individuals described herein, you'll no doubt decide on a favourite. I myself am partial to the exploits of Bernarr Macfadden, a progenitorial physical-fitness guru who used to lug bags of cement, barefoot, to work in the mornings. I also find fascinating William Seabrook, that rascal cannibal who used to go drinking with Aleister Crowley. There's also George Francis Train, who in fact made it around the world in eighty days—not including jail time.

In this collection, you have a vast selection of scalawags, a bevy of scourges, in which to indulge. Just try not to rush through them, however tempting that may be. Jim's stories, like a well-aged scotch, deserve to be sipped, slowly, and enjoyed thoroughly.

—*Cameron Johnson*
Associate Editor, *NUVO Magazine*

# Introduction

In these pages you will encounter gamblers and adventurers, con men and con women, rodomontades and ragamuffins, outright fools and outrageous liars. Scalawags, the lot of them.

But you can be an adventurer, a con man or con woman, a fool, liar, gambler, rodomontade or ragamuffin and not be a scalawag. Many adventurers are not even interesting, come to think of it, let alone scalawags. There is an elusive, indefinable quality—it's downright ineffable, in fact—that sets these people apart, places them in the special category that I call "scalawag." You might call them something else: nuts, perhaps. And quite frankly in many instances—George Francis Train or Louis De Rougemont—you'd probably be right. But likewise you don't have to be a crackpot to be a scalawag: Two Gun Cohen, for instance, or Lady Jane Digby.

What you have to be is outrageous with a bit of what Andre Malraux—an adventurer and liar, perhaps, but not a scalawag—(he's close though. Oh, so close. I mean, whilst serving as Culture Minister during the De Gaulle regime, he convinced the Americans that he knew Chairman Mao personally; in fact, they were good pals, and, consequently, he was flown to Washington to brief President Nixon. Malraux had never even met Chairman Mao but Nixon believed all he said) designated, in reviving an old French word, *farfelu*. It means that you are willing to risk everything, whether on a grand or small scale, on the craziest of schemes, the wildest of notions. Search for the source of the Nile, you're an adventurer. Convince the locals thereabouts to worship you as a king, whether you're an albino or not, you're a scalawag. Catherine of Russia may have been great but Eliza Lynch, who also ruled a kingdom having forsaken high-class whoring, was a scalawag.

Some of them were thieves but not dull kleptomaniacs or two-bit pilferers like Jean Genet or the doper down the street; they were outrageous. So it is with this kind. Sometimes your heart almost breaks for them, you know how it's going to turn out—not well—and maybe they did too but it was out of their hands. They were in the grip of something beyond their control. In the grip of a fever, the fever of *more life*.

You will find that these men and women were scalawag-ish in many spheres of activity. They were soldiers of fortune but also artists, doctors, dancers, comedians, musicians, train robbers and even, believe it or not, writers (Sadakichi Hartmann, Charles Cros). Of course, they were writers at a time when being housebroken was not a prerequisite of the profession.

Can one be a genuine hell-for-leather, crazy-as-a-loon scalawag today?

No.

I'd like to cop out here as is the wont of Adults answering similar questions, like: "Can I really be whatever I want to be?" ("Of course, daughter, if you want it bad enough.") Or, more to our point: "Is it still possible to be an explorer and polymath on the order of Richard Francis Burton?" (No scalawag either, but also close.) "Sure, son. Why not?" But I can't do it. Even Malraux would be embarrassed to tell such whoppers. Hell, you can't whisk with your whiskbroom on a tomb in a graveyard in suburban Indiana without a master's degree in Archaeology. You can't work your way over the pond on a freighter any more, either, what with unions and "security" clearances. Security keeps you away from the docks, even. Security keeps you away from everything. Security's going to get you.

They won't even let you cover a war without "embedding" you. They now know everything you do. They would have twigged to Lola Montez the moment she tried to re-enter the United Kingdom (after "reinventing"—as they say—herself during a sojourn in Spain.) Now, they'll get you with a retinal scan, if all else fails. Trebitsch Lincoln was a man of a hundred identities, and they'd be wise to every one of them. Wilson Mizner sold gangster dialogue to screenwriters from a booth in the Brown Derby, now you have to have a degree in Film Studies from a recognized university before you can even get a screenplay read by another Film Studies graduate. Anyway, gangsters talk like television characters talking like they think gangsters might talk if they weren't talking like their television counterparts.

You can't even run a good old wire store anymore and on Sumatra they know all about albinos and the pigeon drop, they've seen it all on the world wide web. I remember crossing rice paddies in Vietnam, a young man having let me ride atop the family ox, and we came to a place where three women in conical hats were squatting to pick weeds. It was a misty morning, the vaguest outline of a temple in the distance. I heard a melodic chiming of bells, it was so very poetic. I can be forgiven for assuming the music came from the temple. But then one of the women reached into the pocket of her blouse, pulled out a cell phone, and flipped it open, "Ha!"

But just as important in the decline of scalawagishness, is the global financial situation, the absurd increase in the cost of living since the end of the golden age, which lasted from about the dawn of Time, until the mass media takeover of Human Life, circa 1960. The Rich are richer, the Poor are desperately so, and Mr. and Ms. Average are in serious trouble.

Think of any of the scalawags encountered in these pages; he or she pulled into Gotham, tap city and relying on the ankle express but not to worry, all that was needed was a dime for grub, two bits for a flop and tomorrow's another day, a bright new morning to barnyard the dice of life.

But, today, you arrive on a plane, at Vancouver, and it costs you twelve dollars to ride the airport bus into town, ten bucks for a passable meal and ninety bucks for a room with the toilet down the hall. And in ten years, when this book is in its tenth edition, these prices will seem downright quaint.

The notion of a would-be scalawag with empty pockets getting something going by nightfall in these anemic but parlous times is as absurd as a working man or woman getting together, with no help from mommy or daddy, the down payment to buy a house. It's the size of the nut, not the balls.

Conversely, money isn't what it used to be, relatively speaking. One morning, Wilson Mizner might not be holding, as the expression had it, and the next be snug in a four-room suite at the Ritz, having paid in advance with dough he hustled in the past twenty-four hours. The next time he was broke, he just went on the prowl and restored his fortunes in a matter of hours. You just can't swing with that kind of loot in that short a time these days.

One can't escape. But take heart, anyone who would consciously set out to be a scalawag would never have been one, even a hundred years ago. It's not a career goal, it just happens. You are what you are.

One can, however, live to the fullest, as did these people. That's what these scalawags can teach you; just keep your hand on your wallet while you're learning. Mind the words on Mr. Weil's tombstone:

*Here lies the Yellow Kid, underground*
*Don't jingle any change while walking around*

And the last recorded words of the immortal Marcel Horne (which were spoken to me): "There's a ship leaving for the Marquesas tomorrow and I intend to be on it. And I'm not coming back. Put the word around that I was run over and killed by a truck in Gibtown. That's life."

Yes, that's life and there is still hope, and if any further advice is required please send cash or email your credit card number and I'll send you by return mail the entire Scalawags Course, fully approved by the Count de Saint-Germain. Steamer trunk, loaded dice and false whiskers extra. The first thirty-nine people to pay up are afforded the once in a lifetime opportunity to purchase, at the special introductory rate, a two-and-a-half hectare lot off the coast of Irian Jaya, home of legendary licentious dancing girls who like to mingle. No sales people will visit your home.

*—Jim Christy, Toronto, June 2008.*

# Tallulah Bankhead (1902–1968)

She was volcanic. A force of nature, so fiery it seems all wrong that her name is not emblazoned on the culture. How could so much molten personality be damped so soon after her death?

Tallulah Bankhead. Although the name barely resonates now, her influence is all over the place; she left quotes and anecdotes that remain like those figures from the eruption at Pompeii, perpetuated in stone.

Every time you hear one theatre type greet another with an affected, "Dahling!" that's Tallulah Bankhead. When "Ooh"-ing and "Aah"-ing over the great film *All About Eve,* know that it is Tallulah Bankhead whom Bette Davis is playing. All those wonderful Tennessee Williams women? Most, Blanche DuBois foremost among them, are Tallulah Bankhead. "I wrote the whole thing with her in mind," said Williams. "Every word Blanche spoke I heard Tallulah speaking it."

And the quotes!

If Wilson Mizner didn't say it, you can be sure Tallulah did. Compared to her, Dorothy Parker was your garden-variety virago. It was Tallulah, and not Parker, who said, "I'm as pure as the driven slush."

She was famous for, among other things, a husky voice. Broadway columnist Earl Wilson once asked her if she'd ever been mistaken for a man. "No," Tallulah replied. "Have you?"

# 16 | SCALAWAGS

IMAGE COURTESY OF THE LIBRARY OF CONGRESS (1934).

She was born in 1902, near Huntsville, Alabama. Her mother died when she was three weeks old and, consequently, Tallulah would always worship her father, a U.S. Congressman, later Speaker of the House of Representatives. Her grandfather and uncles, all Democrats, had been U.S. Senators. She came from money and liberalism.

Her talents were first acknowledged by, of all people, Wilbur and Orville Wright, who gave her a prize after a recitation. She had a loud voice, a loud style, and liked to play pranks and do imitations.

She got tossed out of one school after another, and as a teenager began to pal around and get into trouble with another local girl, Zelda Sayre, who would marry F. Scott Fitzgerald. It is unclear when Tallulah started drinking but it's certain that she never stopped. She quit school at age fifteen and won a beauty contest sponsored by *Photoplay* magazine. The prize was a screen test in New York.

A promised contract never materialized, but Tallulah stayed on in Manhattan, and at the Algonquin Hotel of all places, the dining room of which surrounded the famous Round Table. There, the young girl held her own, serving her apprenticeship with those notorious and vicious wits. Soon, she was appearing on Broadway in bit parts and making silent films on Long Island. She was also drinking with enthusiasm, taking cocaine, and jumping in and out of bed with whomever was available. Once, at a party, she was seen taking cocaine and kissing another young actress. When a fellow guest remarked about her behaviour, Tallulah responded, "Daddy warned me about men and booze; he didn't say anything about women and cocaine."

One night at the Round Table, after Alexander Woollcott told a story about an early sexual experience, Tallulah remarked, "I was raped in the driveway when I was eleven. It was a terrible experience because of all that gravel."

Encountering Douglas Fairbanks, Jr. on a train with his new wife, Joan Crawford, Tallulah told her: "You know, I've had an affair with your husband. You're next."

In 1923, Tallulah went to England to star in a show called *The Dancers*. She played a music hall hoofer from British Columbia who became a ballerina in Paris. She was a success, and stayed in England for ten years.

It was only in 2003 that Home Office documents were released that reveal Tallulah was investigated throughout those years for seducing Eton schoolboys.

Returning to America in the early '30s, Tallulah got caught up in films, most of them bad. Not yet thirty years old, she was already notorious and found it difficult to rein in her outsized personality, to subjugate it to the role. It didn't help that she seemed unable to tell a good script from a bad one. The audience paid to see Tallulah Bankhead, not a shy cowgirl or put-upon housewife.

Too often, she gave them what they wanted, although there were more than a few glimpses of genius, both on stage and in films.

Her role in Lillian Hellman's *The Little Foxes* was called one of the greatest acting performances ever to be seen on an American stage. She won the Critic's Circle Award for her part in Alfred Hitchcock's *Lifeboat,* although the Motion Picture Academy didn't award her an Oscar.

She toured in *Private Lives* for a year and a half in 1947 and 1948, and was wildly successful—with audiences. Critics panned her performance and the author agreed with them. Noël Coward wrote an open letter to the press, denigrating Tallulah Bankhead, but that didn't stop audiences from packing the theatres. She made the part, originated by Gertrude Lawrence, her own. She did this by satirizing her role, encouraging people to laugh at, rather than with, the play. She was probably right. *Private Lives* is lighthearted and frothy and reserved. It can't cross the water and still keep its distance.

In 1949, Tallulah Bankhead did a screen test for the lead in *The Glass Menagerie.* The director, Irving Rapper, and the crew were in agreement that it was not only the best test for the part but the best screen test they had ever seen. In fact, the cameraman, Karl Freund, wouldn't work the next day. "How can I?" he asked, "after seeing Tallulah?"

But she didn't get the part. It went to Gertrude Lawrence. The decision was made by Jack Warner, who had just lost a small fortune because of Errol Flynn's drinking bouts during his last picture. He said that no matter how great Tallulah was, he couldn't take her and Flynn back to back.

In 1950, she started a three-year stint as mistress of ceremonies of *The Big Show*, a variety program on radio. For ninety minutes she quipped, sang, and introduced America's famous stars. The show not only made her a ton of money, it assured she would never again be taken seriously as an actress.

In 1955, when she finally got to play Blanche Dubois in a revival of *A Streetcar Named Desire,* she had to battle her audiences which were invariably comprised mostly of homosexuals and drag queens who wished to regard every line she uttered as ironic or camp. The reviews were bad. The playwright excoriated the audiences in a letter to *The New York Times,* admitting that he had cried all the way through

Ms. Bankhead's performance and fallen at her feet afterwards. He later wrote that the only thing that thwarted Tallulah was the lack of a strong personality, "a Stanley like Brando or Tony Quinn playing opposite her."

Although Tallulah Bankhead would appear in many other plays and films, in television dramas and soap opera, and as a guest on talk shows, she never again extended herself creatively during the last thirteen years of her life. It hardly seems possible, but she lived even more outrageously. The parties lasted longer. She couldn't bear to be alone. She treated everyone equally; at her gatherings were Hollywood stars, politicians, and beggars from the street.

One of the last times she left her apartment was to attend Truman Capote's masked ball at the Plaza Hotel. *The New York Times* had published the guest list, and when she pulled up to the Plaza in a limousine, there was a crowd of fans hollering, "Tallulah, we love you!"

A few weeks later, she went to Marlene Dietrich's one-woman show at the Lunt-Fontanne Theatre. It must have hurt Tallulah, racked by emphysema, ravaged by booze and insomnia, to see Dietrich, one year older than her, not only still beautiful but triumphant on stage.

After two television appearances in California, on *Batman* and *The Smothers Brothers,* Tallulah returned to her apartment in New York, and resumed her regimen of soap operas, cigarettes, and booze. One visitor said Tallulah looked like she had been repeatedly thrown against the wall.

She died of pneumonia on December 12, 1968. People who'd been close to her were a little surprised that the lights didn't go out and that the world kept turning. It wasn't right that the volcano was extinguished; maybe she's just dormant. §

# William Beckford (1760–1844)

ETCHING BY J. WILKES, LONDON 1798. BEINECKE RARE BOOK AND MANUSCRIPT LIBRARY, YALE UNIVERSITY.

In 1781, William Beckford, considered the wealthiest man in England, celebrated his majority with a three-day festival that would never be called a party, rather a bacchanalia or orgy, at his country house in Wiltshire. Beckford was at the time engaged in a torrid affair with the lady next door, that door being far away from his own, and the lady being the wife of his cousin. Louise Beckford was married with children, but together they schemed that she might stay away for the entire length of the party, or longer. "Stay a week, then we must lie in wait for souls together," Beckford wrote and in reply was told, "—my lovely infernal! How gloriously you write of iniquities...like another Lucifer you would tempt Angels to forsake their celestial abode, and sink with you in the black infernal gulph."

Not content with Louisa by herself, William arranged for the primary object of his affection, another neighour known as Kitty, to also sleep over. He had been in love with Kitty for two years, a love yet to be consummated. It would be consummated on Beckford's birthday in a ménage à trois.

Beckford spent a fortune on the celebrations, even hiring Philippe de Loutherbourg, chief set designer at David Garrick's Drury Lane Theatre, to decorate his mansion and present a show with his new invention, the *Eidophusikon,* a moving picture machine. Loutherbourg was the perfect choice for this particular job; not only was he considered a genius, but he had also been forced to flee France as the consequence of sexual scandal. Both William and Phillippe had vast libraries of mysticism, were Freemasons, and practiced a system of testicular meditation, the purpose of which was the prolongation of intercourse.

The celebration was a great success. Guests were overwhelmed by Beckford's home from the moment the master's chief servant, a dwarf, opened the massive brass front doors. One reveler, attempting to describe Loutherbourg's show and decorations, coined a phrase that would lie dormant for two hundred years, saying that the atmosphere was a "virtual reality."

In the midst of the celebration and her raptures, Louisa vowed to leave her husband and children for Beckford. Kitty, in turn, enthusiastically succumbed to Beckford's advances. In one sense, then, the orgy was most fulfilling; in another, for Beckford, it would have tragic consequences. Kitty was now only thirteen years old; what is more, Kitty was a male. His name was William Courtenay, and his uncle, Lord Loughborough, was a chief justice. This worthy representative of the crown, evidently a noted conservative bigot, found out about the affair and publicly announced the scandal, running the ill-starred couple's love letters in the newspapers over the course of three months.

Beckford had to leave Great Britain until, he thought, the whole thing would blow over; alas, it never did.

William was one of numerous children sired by a father who was known as Alderman Beckford. Twelve years a member of Parliament and twice Lord Mayor of London, the Alderman owned plantations covering seven thousand acres in Jamaica. Of all his offspring, William was the only legitimate one. The elder died when William was twelve years old, leaving him £100 sterling and an annual income of £100,000 sterling.

By then the boy had already exhibited interests in art, architecture, poetry, and music. At the latter he seemed to be quite gifted. A story developed that William took piano lessons from Wolfgang Amadeus Mozart. In later years, many dismissed the story; in reality, however, the two did meet and Mozart gave Beckford some pointers—Mozart was eight years old and Beckford five. Twenty years later, Beckford boasted that he gave Mozart one of the tunes in *The Marriage of Figaro*.

Beckford's godfather and guardian was Sir William Chambers, who encouraged his love of architecture, as did his Russian-born art tutor, Alexander Cozzens. Together they decorated Fonthill's entrance-way; in Beckford's words it was a "Hall of the Pyramid...blowing with yellow light amid vases from another Hemisphere and Cabalistic Mirrors wherein Futurity is unveiled." He was seventeen at the time.

His education was directed by other tutors and music teachers. He read omnivorously, though mainly in the classics and works about the oriental world. His favourite book was *The Arabian Nights*. His early life was one of privilege and self-indulgence; so was his later life.

After the scandal, Beckford left on a grand tour, and grand it was. He was followed by five coaches and a retinue of servants. At one point he was mistaken for the Emperor of Austria. Beckford even had his own painter to record great scenes of Europe, usually with him posed imperiously in the foreground. In Lisbon, Beckford hired six musicians to play for and with him, and remarked, "These Portuguese youths are composed of more inflammable materials than other mortals." One in particular had him on fire, a "sweet-breathed" harpsichordist named Gregorio Franchi who was seventeen, and "a very faithful animal strenuously attached to me."

When they were apart, Beckford liked to prop himself up with cushions and "whilst the music...play[ed] a slow and melancholy strain, folded my arms, closed my eyes, and fancied I beheld Franchi."

But there were other cities and other "youths."

In Paris, shortly after the fall of the Bastille, Beckford was arrested as an English spy and was able to escape and flee due to the help of the famous book dealer Chardin, whom he would reward with a pension.

When, after a few years, he returned to England and Wiltshire, Beckford devoted himself to remaking his country home, composing operas, dallying with his young male servants—there were usually thirty of these—and writing a gothic and homoerotic novel called *Vahtek*. Much has been made of this work and its influence on writers as diverse as Huysmans, Disraeli, and Byron, who, in *Childe Harold's Pilgrimage*, mentions *Vahtek*. When he was only eighteen years old, Beckford penned an even more original book called *Biographical Memoirs of Extraordinary Painters*, which was a totally fictitious work about artists he insisted were real. A few years later, Beckford published *Dreams, Waking Thoughts, and Incidents*, a sort of stream of consciousness travel book. His friends managed to stop a second printing because of Beckford's fulsome descriptions of sexual encounters.

Beckford, who was opposed to blood sports, had a twelve-foot-high stone wall built around his property. The wall was eleven miles long. There is, however, no record of his having given a thought to the living conditions of his hundreds of slaves in Jamaica. His foremost achievement was the building of Fonthill Abbey with its three-hundred-foot tower. He got rid of most of his inherited possessions and furnished the rebuilt house with his collections. He was eventually reckoned to have the greatest art and antique collections in England. He had several paintings by Giovanni Bellini, Titians, a Canaletto, Hogarth's *A Rake's Progress*, three paintings by Rembrandt, and dozens of others. As well, he owned Greek vases and Japanese lacquered boxes.

Beckford went frequently to the continent to visit the homosexual underworld and to add to his collections. On one of these trips he became friends with Gasparo Pacchierotti, a castrato known as a great counter-tenor, and accompanied him on a singing tour of Italy. On another trip, in Venice, Beckford met Augusta Wynne, who is mentioned in Casanova's memoirs. He soon wrote a piece for piano and voice, *Aria for Sgra Wynne*. But there is more to this gesture than mere flattery. Augusta, like her aunt Catherine, was a sort of upper class procurer, and she arranged for Beckford an alliance with the brother of two poor sisters for whom she had been finding rich Lords. With this boy, he experienced "delirium," which was his code word for sexual delight.

Incredibly, for two years after returning to England from his first grand tour, Beckford was married, and devoted, to Lady Margaret Gordon. She died giving birth to their second daughter. He had his children raised in another building on the estate. Throughout his marriage and after, Beckford continued to wonder about the love of his life, Kitty, who had gone into exile. He referred to Kitty as a "she" in letters to his cousin Louisa: "does she love to talk of the hour when, seizing her delicate hand, I led her bounding like a kid to my chamber…Is she not mine? Will I ever again be happy?"

He made do with his journeys, his architectural experiments and his servants who served in many capacities.

The first of Beckford's towers fell down after five years. He subsequently employed five hundred masons to work around the clock to build another one so that he could keep his head literally where it had always been figuratively: in the clouds. This too crumbled. The third tower collapsed in 1825, after which Beckford moved to Bath. He bought two houses and connected them with an archway over which was an apartment. He also erected another tower 154 feet high, at the foot of which was his sarcophagus of rose-coloured granite. He spent much of his time at the top of the tower alone with his fantasies.

Often Beckford rode about on his white Arabian stallion. Stories developed about him and the mysterious activities in his houses. It was said that he practiced black magic and devil worship. It was true that the apartment over the archway was occupied by several dwarves.

When finally it came time to occupy his sarcophagus, Beckford had lived eighty-two years. He was in vigorous health until his death.

One can easily imagine him, an old satyr, riding his stallion, or coming to the front gate in hopes of spying some comely youth. §

# John Romulus Brinkley (1885–1942)

In 1913 John Romulus Brinkley was nothing but a cheap grafter, a cheque kiter, and medicine-show hustler, trying his hand at medical charlatanism in Milford, a god-forsaken town of 150 people in Kansas, when a farmer walked into his office and changed his life forever. After he was done with the farmer, Brinkley was on his way to becoming the richest medical practitioner in North America, if not the world; the man who would, before he died thirty-five years later, also revolutionize what was then a communications baby in swaddling clothes: radio. As well, Brinkley would drag advertising into the modern era and take country music out of the hills and present it to the world.

Brinkley knew about those hills—he was born in them in North Carolina in 1885, and it is so very fitting, given his future, that his mother was his aunt. His father's wife was evidently worn out by drudgery, but her sister was young and comely. John's father scraped a living out of the rocky land and was a rural doctor on the side. Being a rural doctor at the time meant that one had worked for an older rural doctor who himself had trained the same way. What one learned and administered was basically folk medicine.

John Brinkley married in 1907, and accompanied by his young wife, Sally, went out on the road with his own medicine show. They dressed the way they thought Quakers dressed and, after some non-

JOHN R. BRINKLEY. COURTESY OF THE KANSAS STATE HISTORICAL SOCIETY.

Quaker-like song and dance numbers, peddled their "elixir" for whatever ailed you, from cancer to whooping cough to flagging sexual energy. Some of the little bottles that went for a dollar each were brown-coloured water, others blue-coloured water.

Brinkley spent several years rushing from one town to the next, usually no more than a step ahead of the law. His wanderings are impossible to trace, as are his attempts at studying medicine. By claiming a high school degree he hadn't earned, Brinkley got into something called The Milton Academy, which purported to be a medical school.

At the time there was no standardized medical training and doctors who had any schooling whatsoever fell into two camps: Regulars and Irregulars. The former were allopaths who believed in treating disease with drugs that produced symptoms opposite those of the illness. Homeopaths, the most popular of the irregulars, treated patients with drugs that produced similar symptoms. Osteopaths maintained that illness was caused by problems in the blood or nervous systems. Eclectics held that herbs could heal most complaints. The allopaths eventually came to dominate, despite a predilection for mercury treatments and for bleeding patients.

Not surprisingly, John Brinkley went with the eclectics. The schools of the major sects taught many of the same courses, in chemistry, pathology, and anatomy. Brinkley did attend classes at Milton for three years but left when he could no longer pay tuition. He found a diploma mill in St. Louis called The National University of Arts and Sciences, and bought a paper that stated he had earned a medical degree. In 1912, Brinkley, after a spell working with another quack purporting to treat gonorrhea and syphilis, met a grafter of higher attainments. It was in a bar in Memphis (John Brinkley was a serious boozer), and the man, one James Crawford, had perpetrated his schemes all over the world. The pair moved to Greenville, South Carolina, rented an office and proclaimed themselves "Electro Medic Doctors." They posed a question in a local newspaper ad: "Are You a Manly Man Full of Vigor?"

The two were soon doing a lucrative trade restoring manly vigor at twenty-five dollars a bottle (of coloured distilled water). Crawford had been around enough to sense when the law was closing in and eventually did a moonlight flit. Brinkley didn't split until the next morning, and barely escaped the minions of the law.

The pair of con men had a coincidental meeting in a jailhouse sometime later. Brinkley was arrested in Knoxville for practicing medicine without a license; Crawford was incarcerated for unpaid bills.

Crawford had once introduced Brinkley to a Georgia girl and doctor's daughter named Minerva Telitha Jones. They were married in 1913. John neglected to tell her that he was already married.

This, then, was the kind of man who had been in Milford, Kansas for exactly two weeks when that farmer, one William Stitsworth, came into his office. Mr William Stittsworth never discussed the operation that Brinkley performed on him that day, and it wasn't until some sixty years later that a view contrary to the one in Brinkley's biography (he hired the writer) was expressed. According to the biography, Stittsworth told Brinkley that he was impotent and suggested the doctor give him some glands from a healthy goat. Brinkley supposedly thought the man was—according to the biographer whose work displayed no other bit of humour or irony—"nuts."

Brinkley's only previous experience with goats was as a meat inspector at the Swift Plant in Kansas City. He had, however, made a cursory study of gland transplantation such as was being done in Europe. Brinkley did the transplant and, lo and behold, whether through miracle or suggestion, the formerly impotent farmer soon impregnated his wife, and their baby, Billy, was born ten months after the operation. It was Billy who, in the '70s, supplied the other version of the story. Stittsworth, Billy claimed, had gone to Brinkley with prostrate trouble. The doctor convinced him to have a goat gland transplant. Two weeks later, Brinkley asked Stittsworth, "Help you any?" Stittsworth replied, "Damn right. Got my wife pregnant."

No matter where the truth lay, Stittsworth was restored to manly vigor and Brinkley was on his way. Soon he had to build a hospital to accommodate the patients. In the middle of the Depression, Brinkley and his colleagues were doing fifty goat gland transplants a day, five days a week, at $750 per; there was also a special compound operation for $1,000. As well, Brinkley was big on prostate operations. Soon he owned half the town, drove around in Cadillacs and Lincolns, and started his own radio station.

In the late 1920s, the American Medical Association started a file on Brinkley because so many of its members had lost business to him. It sent private detectives throughout the country to amass information. But the campaign didn't go public until a series of articles condemning Brinkley appeared in *The Kansas City Star*. The result was that his medical license was revoked, but he still operated his hospital.

Eventually he lost his radio license for prescribing medicine over the air. Brinkley's response was to travel to Villa Acuña, Mexico, put up massive transmitters and start broadcasting over a new station, XER. Over the next ten years, under various call letters, the station was a carnival sideshow on the airwaves, and, with its one million watts, could be heard all throughout the Americas from Argentina to the Northwest Territories. The Carter Family, Gene Autry, Roy Rogers, Red Foley and Little Jimmy Dickens all got their start singing live on XER. But the most popular act was Rose Dawn, who sold horoscopes and gave advice to the lovelorn. She was married to a guy who called himself Koran, a missionary for the Mayan Order.

Brinkley had set up another hospital across the Rio Grande in Del Rio, Texas. From October 1933 to January 1938, he and his staff operated on sixteen thousand patients, earning twelve million dollars. In addition, Brinkley had radio income—he was selling ads by then—and dozens of other investments, including a goat farm in Oklahoma.

There are some who state that although Brinkley was a paranoid megalomaniac with delusions of grandeur, he was also an entrepreneur and weird genius who might have done genuine good in the world if he wasn't so twisted. Maybe so, but one has to fear the do-gooders as much as the charlatans. Also, if he hadn't been so twisted, one wouldn't think of him every time the radio is turned on, whether to a country tune, a corny ad, or a sexologist. And then there is the story just read in a serious newspaper about an amazing new treatment for depression that consists of the doctor placing an electric tube on the patient's head to stimulate the frontal lobe. At least Dr. John only took you for a few dollars, and he was funny too. §

# Ned Buntline (1821 – 1886)

Ned Buntline is usually portrayed in the movies as a bespectacled little scribbler from back east, in ridiculous plaid suits, pen in hand, and more than a little intimidated to be listening to the tales of steely-eyed heroes of the Wild West. Back to New York City he'd scurry, with tales he'd inflate to Homeric proportions in paperback productions known as dime novels.

Well, a good part of all that is true. He was from back east and wasn't all that tall. Inflate the stories of these men he certainly did, had to do, because most of them were little more than trail bums—sort of slackers of the old West—but intimidated? Well, by the time he found a certain part-time Indian scout lying under a wagon in Nebraska and decided to make him a hero, Buntline had already served in four wars, been a scout himself, shipped around the world a dozen times before he was seventeen, been arrested more times than he could count, had a dozen knife and bullet wounds, been married numerous times and often simultaneously, been in duels, and he'd even been hanged in Tennessee. Oh, yes, and he'd published three hundred novels. His name wasn't even Ned Buntline.

So when he pulled William Frederick Cody out from under that wagon at North Platte, Nebraska in August 1869, he was not the sort to be intimidated by any man, especially not by a kid who'd been in the Civil War but seen no action and had only recently been employed

AUTHOR EDWARD ZANE CARROLL JUDSON (NED BUNTLINE), A MILITARY OFFICER DURING THE AMERICAN CIVIL WAR. PHOTOGRAPHED BY MATHEW B. BRADY, CIRCA 1861. USED WITH PERMISSION. © MEDFORD HISTORICAL SOCIETY COLLECTION/CORBIS.

by the Army to shoot buffalo. Hell, Cody wasn't even the man Ned had wanted; it was Major Frank North he was interested in, a legendary scout and the man who'd recently killed the Cheyenne chief Tall Bull. But the taciturn North wanted no part of the pushy little man and directed Ned to Cody. Well, the kid looked the part. At first, the local layabouts and rounders thought the easterner was full of it with his outrageous stories, but they stopped doubting him when they saw that Ned could ride and shoot as well as, if not better than, any of them.

Buntline did go back to New York, where he transformed the good-looking kid into a hero under the moniker of Buffalo Bill. When half the households in the United States knew this new Apollo's name—which didn't take long—Buntline put him on stage. The rest is that old synonym for "a pack of lies": history.

The man called Ned Buntline put James Hickok on stage too, but Wild Bill, the real deal, walked away from it all in disgust.

Anyway, that Buffalo Bill gaffe was just a passing fancy in the little man's career. He'd been invited out west in the first place by a temperance society to give lectures. Not that Buntline was anti-alcohol; he was, in fact, a prodigious boozer; but he was also a spell-binding speaker and made good money at it. The underlying intention of his western trip was to ride east in the first train to cross the continent and write about it for the papers, but he got drunk and missed the train.

Edward Zane Carroll Judson was born in either Pennsylvania or New York State sometime between 1820-1823. He spent most of his childhood alone in the woods of Western Pennsylvania. He ran away to sea as a cabin boy when he was twelve, using 1823 as his year of birth, and shipped to Rio de Janeiro. At fourteen, he enlisted in the Navy and was languishing at the base in Brooklyn when he rescued three other sailors from drowning and was awarded a commission. After a tour of duty in the Caribbean, Judson began service in the Seminole Wars in Florida where he was wounded and given a medal. At the age of seventeen, he was married in Havana, Cuba, and had his first story published in the leading literary journal of its day, *The Knickerbocker*.

Although he would write lyric poetry the rest of his life, Judson realized early on that he'd never make a living at serious prose, so he turned to the rich material of his youth for stories. He took his pseudonym from the length of rope that hangs down from a main mast, the buntline. He would later publish under a dozen pseudonyms, among them Charlie Bowline and Edward Clewline, as well as that distinguished handle: Edward J. C. Handelboe.

He roamed around the Midwest starting magazines and getting in trouble. More than once, when his magazine floundered, Buntline did a moonlight flit, leaving his partners to pay the debts. He occasionally had to lam from town on account of angry husbands. But he was a hero, too, receiving a large cash award in Eddyville, Kentucky for capturing two dangerous killers. This event occurred a week or so after his first wife, Seberina, died. Not long afterward, he was hanged in Nashville.

Buntline had been keeping clandestine company with one Mary Porterfield, who was nineteen, beautiful, and married. She and Buntline had been less than discreet and her husband, Robert, went looking for the ink-stained wretch. He found Buntline and fired six shots at him, grazing him twice. Buntline fired back once and sent a bullet into Porterfield's skull above the left eye. Porterfield's friends took him to the doctor and Buntline surrendered to the law. At the trial, Buntline pleaded self-defense and all witnesses concurred. Before he was acquitted, however, Porterfield's brother, along with a gang of men, burst into the courthouse and opened fire on Buntline, who went through the window. Running across the street to a hotel, he was hit in the chest with a bullet, and in the head with a stone thrown by a youth. The mob cornered him on the third floor of the hotel, and again Buntline exited via a window. He grabbed for a coping, missed, and fell forty-seven feet to the ground. He was picked up and carried to the jail. Later that night, when it was learned that Porterfield had died, the mob broke into the jail, dragged Buntline out into the street and strung him up by the neck from an awning post. A battle ensued between the Porterfield gang and Buntline's friends—with little Ned hanging there. Finally he was cut down and spirited away until a new trial could be held. Eventually, Buntline was acquitted. And that's how he got to New York.

There he started another magazine and published more dime novels, including *The Red Revenger* and *The Black Avenger*, the pirate Tom Sawyer dreamed of being in his *Adventures*.

There was another wife, a couple more jails and a dozen novels in the two years that followed his flight from Nashville. Then in 1849, he was sent to prison over his complicity in starting the famous Astor Place Riot on May 10. There had been feuding for years between English and American actors. Every time the American Edwin Forrest and his English rival William Charles Macready appeared there was controversy in the press and confrontation outside the theatres. The rivalry intensified and led to the riot outside the Astor Place Opera House after Macready played Macbeth. Buntline was extremely anti-British, an unusual stance since his wife was English and they lived in the house of her English father.

Buntline was arrested and held in jail for several days before posting bond. The next ten days are typical in the life of the man. Waiting for him on the steps of the jail were two process servers. One handed him a summons to appear as defendant in a slander suit brought against him by publisher James Gordon Bennett. The other represented his wife in a case for divorce. Buntline walked away with the papers in hand only to be picked up a block later and clapped in jail for non-payment of a debt to a firm of ship chandlers. Once free, he himself brought suit against a former employee who wrote a book about him. He didn't appear in court in the matter of the ship chandlers so the court seized his yacht and were going to put it up for auction, but Buntline and his crew stole aboard and sailed away. After several days at sea, the yacht put ashore at Philadelphia and the captain repaired to a saloon, sauntered up to the bar and shouted, "Set 'em up, I'm Ned Buntline, hero of a hundred fights!"

The number was soon to be one-hundred-one because another drinker took exception to his braggadocio. Unfortunately for Ned, the fellow was a foot taller and fifty pounds heavier, and heaved Buntline out the swinging doors and into the gutter.

A couple of weeks later, Buntline was sentenced to a year's hard labour at Blackwell's Island. He looked as if he'd lived a difficult forty-six years but was, in fact, only twenty-six.

Upon his release, Buntline headed for St. Louis where he immediately got involved in an election riot and was jailed again. He was let out on bail and failed to show up for his trial. Twenty years later, while appearing in a play in St. Louis with Buffalo Bill and Texas Jack Omohundro, Buntline was picked up and held on the old charge.

A couple of years are missing from the chronology but it seems that Buntline disappeared into the west, crossing the prairies and the Rockies and making his way to California. All the time, he was writing more novels and stories under his various pseudonyms.

By the late 1850s, he was living with a new wife in a homemade cabin in the Adirondack Mountains. After that wife left with their baby, Buntline married Anna Fuller, who'd be his last wife and who soon bore him another child. He lived by writing, and by hunting and fishing. Eventually Buntline showed up in Stamford, New York where he set up in a tent on the edge of town. He enlisted in the Union Army in 1862, and served with some distinction as a scout and taught his fellow soldiers—all younger than he—woodcraft. He later claimed to have dispatched many of the enemy. In the winter of 1862 he went to Manhattan on leave, divided his time between his wife, his sweetheart, and various fancy houses and neglected to return to camp by the appropriate date. He was tried for desertion and thrown into Norfolk Prison.

In 1864, he was released and spent several months on a spree in New York. One day Mathew Brady photographed him, drunk, in a Colonel's uniform, standing beside the same chair where Abraham Lincoln had sat for his portrait.

Friends hardly recognized Buntline. He limped along like an old man, pain from his broken bones and gunshot wounds had caught up with him and competed with sciatica and other ailments. But everything he did turned into an adventure or a misadventure. Drunk, he fell into New York Harbour, only to be rescued by a troupe of actors returning to their rooming house from the theatre. They dried him off and took him to dinner where he regaled them all with stories, some true, others not, although no one could tell the difference. Decades later some of these actors would write about that glorious night.

In 1869, he went west and discovered Buffalo Bill. In 1874, he was out in the badlands again. He'd had special guns made and presented them to notorious figures like Wyatt Earp, Bat Masterson and Bill Tilghman. They were Colt six-shooters with special twelve-inch barrels. Each gun had "Ned" carved into the walnut handle and came with a buckskin rig and a carved holster. The gun entered history as the "Buntline special."

His last ten years were spent fighting illness and ex-wives, writing for outdoors magazines, roaming the East Coast on his Hambletonian mare, and being interviewed by reporters. He died in his sleep in 1886, somewhere between sixty-three and sixty-six years old. It is a matter of Stamford, New York history that Buntline's horse, which had followed his casket with its master's boots backwards in the stirrups, began to cry and scream when it reached the grave site. After the casket was lowered into the grave and covered over, the horse pawed frantically at the dirt. It had been a hell of a ride. §

# Richard Myrle Buckley
## AKA Lord Buckley
## (1906–1960)

In her terrific autobiography *High Times, Hard Times*, Anita O'Day, the jazz singer without vibrato, describes standing in the wings at a nightclub in Chicago and watching the act that she was to follow. The fellow wore a tuxedo and sported a racetrack tout's moustache. The man was not a singer, dancer, or comedian. He talked and talked some more, in a jive language mostly of his own devising. Then, in the middle of his monologue, the man started climbing a beam, and when he reached the rafters, he pulled out a marijuana cigarette, lit it, and continued talking while taking great big inhalations.

Another commentator has him finishing an act with a little speech: "Before I leave you, I'd like to say to you, PEOPLE are what it is all about . . . they are Mother Nature's brightest flower, her sweetest, purest most elevating thing that ever was. You are groovy flowers in a garden where I am privileged to stand and share a few moments with you."

That speech sounds now like your typical platitudinous maunderings mouthed by some bland hippie before he cranks up the guitar at a festival to save the whales; the former incident might capture a performance artist in situ. Both of them could be happening tonight or tomorrow. Thing is, the latter speech was given

IMAGE: ALBUM COVER FOR "THE WAY OUT HUMOR OF LORD BUCKLEY". WORLD PACIFIC RECORDS, 1959 (LIVE CONCERT RECORDING).

after a show at a hotel in Las Vegas in 1954 and the former was observed in Chicago in 1934. Both incidents illustrate that Richard Myrle Buckley, a former logger, was not only decades outside his time, he was untamable and unclassifiable. Some other way lies fame and fortune; his way lies legend.

No one is sure about when devotees started calling him "Lord Buckley." Not many people are sure about anything to do with the man. In his book *Jazz Lives*, Barry Ullman called Lord Buckley "the black comedian and social commentator." Of course, he was not really a comedian and his social commentary was incidental; he wasn't black either. What he was was thoroughly unique, unlike anyone else before or since.

This is a man whose admirers range from Al Capone to Frank Zappa, Elvis Presley to Henry Miller, Whoopi Goldberg to Ed Sullivan. Some have tried to place him in a rebel pantheon but the man wasn't rebelling against anyone or anything, he was just being who he was—His Lordship.

He was born in 1906, the youngest of ten children, in Tuolumne, an old mining town in California. As a young man, he quit a logging job to go to Mexico and work in the oilfields. In Galveston, he met a musician who had a gig at a place called The Million Dollar Aztec Theatre. The musician, entranced by Buckley's monologues on the rooming house porch in the evenings, got him a job at the theatre. Buckley bombed. The manager of the place told him he was "the lousiest act I ever put on in my life."

Buckley later said, "He was right." And went out to pay his dues. He got on the vaudeville circuit and then became an emcee at dance marathons during the Depression. Soon he was working in radio and in small clubs as an entr'acte between the jazz musicians. Some time in the late 1930s, he began working in clubs backed by the Mob. Al Capone took a liking to Buckley and set him up with his own joint. Capone later said, "Buckley is the only person who can make me laugh."

All this time, Buckley was not only gaining experience, he was learning language. He had always loved language, the sounds and rhythms of it. Now he was hearing show business lingo, the argot of jazz, criminal slang, and he absorbed it just as he had the language of loggers as he was growing up and setting out on his own. All of this, in pre-television days, was the talk of subcultures, alternate ways of speaking to that of the dominant society. Buckley took what he liked from all of these and soon had an argot of his own.

And during all this experience, he listened to stories. He listened to them in the woods at night, backstage in small towns, in entertainers' boarding houses, in dressing rooms while a bottle or a joint was passed around. Language and stories became his instrument.

There were plenty of people who didn't appreciate what he was doing—for no other reason than because they'd never heard anything like it—and he was booed off many a stage. People who traveled with him remembered how Buckley would want to stop at a diner with a strange name, might become transfixed by the man working the grille, or by the story one truck driver was telling another one.

And all this time, he was followed by trouble. A lot of it was woman trouble, much of it was law trouble. He went through five or six wives until he hooked up with a former chorus girl named Elizabeth Hanson, soon to be known as Lady Buckley. They were married in 1945, not long after Buckley's one and only pot bust. Forty years after Buckley's death she was still referring to him as His Lordship. "He spoke to everybody. They would wait for him and his invisible dog. He was inspiring to be with."

It was Elizabeth who urged him to work his backstage stories into his act. Soon he was gracing audiences with what he called his "raps," long takes on people such as Mahatma Gandhi ("The Hip Gan"), William Shakespeare ("Willie the Shake"), Álvar Núñez Cabeza de Vaca ("The Gasser"), The Marquis de Sade ("The King of the Bad Cats"). And then there was Jesus Christ, Himself.

And that's who he was talking about when I first heard him in the late 1960s. It was in the wee small hours, radio on, roofs of the city in the window, the booming baritone voice black-inflected and jazz-inspired: "Now lookit here all you cats and kitties out there whippin' and wailin' and jumpin' up and down and suckin' up all that juice and pattin' each other on the back and hippin' each other who the greatest cat in the world is…I'm gonna put a cat on you was the coolest, grooviest, sweetest, wailingest, strongest, swingest cat that ever stomped this jumpin' green sphere. And they called this here cat …the Nazz." And thus followed the tale of the wigged-out dude from Nazareth.

It was just so great and different from anything else anyone was doing, had done, and will do. There are plenty of people who have copied Lord Buckley, and some of them do it well, but the power is not there because the imitators are products of their times. The Lord was doing it in the 1930s and '40s.

His former manager, George Grieff, remembers a party at the

Buckley flat in Manhattan in the early '50s where The Lord was talking and Lenny Bruce and Charlie Parker were sitting at his feet.

Twenty-five years later, Grieff met George Harrison, and when the latter heard he'd been The Lord's manager, the former Beatle began to ply Grieff with questions about Buckley—later, to recite Buckley routines.

Harrison wrote a song about Lord Buckley called "Crackerbox Palace" that has the line "the Lord is well and inside of you." Harrison would later comment, "I meant Lord Buckley but everybody thought I was talking about the other Lord."

And there was the time Buckley had the entire circus at his apartment for a party, and when the cops came, he got them drunk. The time he marched through the lobby of the Sheraton with a dozen naked Hawaiians. Or when he presided at the Church of the Living Swing in Hollywood; everybody sat on railroad ties while Buckley performed to jazz, and there was the first ever light show in America.

Buckley had a small place in the hills called The Mattress Factory, a ramshackle joint open to all at all hours where you were liable to see Rosalind Russell and Jonathan Winters sharing a mattress with a bag lady and James Dean while Buckley talked. Lord Buckley experimented with LSD in 1959.

The next year, about to open at a club in New York, his cabaret license was revoked because of that pot bust back in the '40s. The infamous Cabaret Law was devised and used to persecute jazz musicians and every other entertainer of that ilk. You could have been convicted of murder and your card would not be taken, but one toke of marijuana and that was it. Buckley was so upset by the incident that he had a heart attack and died.

At least, his corporeal form may have ceased to exist. The rest of him, the best of him, will always live on as the swingingest scalawag that ever trod the boards. §

# Joseph Balsamo AKA Count di Cagliostro (1743–1795)

One thing about the Age of Reason is that all those reasonable types seem to have been at the mercy of every charlatan, con man, bogus spiritual leader, snake-oil salesman, and pie-in-the-sky dreamer to come down the pike. The 17$^{th}$ century was, in fact, so outrageous that one cannot help but feel sorry for all the hustlers condemned to exist on either side of it. For all anyone knows, the greatest con man of all time may have been some guy born two hundred years after Cagliostro, some guy who dealt three-card monte on a blanket at the back of his station wagon in an alley in Cleveland; born, in other words, in the wrong era. We'll never know. And since we won't, Cagliostro will just have to take the cake—and the money.

Joseph Balsamo was born in 1743, and to a lot of people interested in these matters—Orson Welles, for instance—he was the greatest of all time. Other cognoscenti come down on the side of the Comte de Sainte Germaine. It is a moot point, but interesting to note, that the two men met in 1770, when Balsamo, fleeing a scandal—he was always fleeing a scandal—called on the elderly St. Germaine (some say he was two thousand years old) at his castle in Sleswig. One can imagine the two scalawags, the powdered-wig veteran and the cocky, young, nimble-fingered dreamer, sitting around cutting up jackpots

IMAGE: PORTRAIT PRINT. ARTIST UNKNOWN. DIBNER LIBRARY PORTRAIT COLLECTION, SMITHSONIAN INSTITUTE.

like a couple of degenerate carnies. Anyway, Balsamo was imbued with a sense of the great hustling possibilities of life. The Comte told him, among other things, to drop all his aliases and stick to one. That way a legend could attach. Balsamo left Sleswig calling himself Count di Cagliostro and wanting a castle of his own.

He was born Joseph Balsamo in Palermo, Sicily. His father died when he was an infant and he was shifted around between relatives of his destitute mother. He spent his teenage years in a convent where he developed a reputation for viciousness. As soon as he could get out of the convent, he began his hustling, beginning with petty forgery and petty thievery. His first jail time was served for forging a will. When a man he had robbed of sixty ounces of gold vowed Sicilian revenge, Balsamo crossed the waters to North Africa.

Somewhere in Arabia he got hooked up with a Greek scholar of the occult, an alchemist and multilinguist named Altotas, who hired Balsamo as his assistant. The Greek was so dedicated to his manuscripts that he had insufficient time to tend to his experiments. While the Greek studied, Balsamo learned his way around a laboratory. The two men soon became partners. The Greek, while trying to turn base metals into gold, had stumbled on a process that rendered materials of flax nearly as soft and shiny as silk. Balsamo advised the Greek that they should hit the road and truly make gold of the flax.

They did, and wandered all over the Middle East, profiting from the flax, visiting the pyramids, and meeting all sorts of caliphs, temple-priests, Rosicrucians, Freemasons, card sharps, prestidigitators, and natural healers. The oriental adventure lasted four years and provided the Palermo street urchin with a priceless education in arcana. Just as significantly, the four years were spent beyond the reach of prying European eyes. The future Cagliostro could weave all sorts of flamboyant tales out of this gaudy material and no one would be the wiser. Hell, he could tell any kind of story he wished. And he did.

When Altotas died in Malta, Balsamo continued his wandering. In Naples, he opened a casino, the sole purpose of which was to separate wealthy foreign tourists from their money. The authorities soon kicked him out of town. In Rome, Balsamo set himself up as a doctor. Something in him had been stirred by the sight of natural healers and faith healers he'd seen on his travels.

While on his medical rounds in Rome, he met a fourteen-year-old girl name Lorenza Felciana. They fell in love and were married. Balsamo was twenty-five. No sooner was the honeymoon over than Balsam had to flee the Inquisition which suspected him of heresy. The couple headed east and spent four years in Russia and Poland.

The young man, Count di Cagliostro by now, had been doing pretty well with his various hustles, but he'd soon realized that his young wife was a con man's dream come true. People were transfixed by her beauty, but she was also educated and had perfect manners. She also had no scruples. If Cagliostro was possibly the ultimate con man, Lorenza was the shill *non pareil*. She reeled the suckers in and the suckers gave her husband the money. Their marks were, of course, from the upper classes. Memoirs of the time are filled with notes like this from an Austrian baroness: "Cagliostro's wife came to call. She is the most beautiful woman we have ever seen...his eyes are indescribable with supernatural depths . . . possessed of a demonic power. He enthralled the mind, paralyzed the will."

Some pair.

He was not, as might be suspected, above serving as her pimp when the john was rich enough and could be drawn into other cons, like a little adventure with necromancy or relief from an incurable affliction. But Cagliostro wasn't staying celibate. He took up with Catherine the Great, who evidently allowed him to dabble in affairs of state. Their affair lasted for several weeks, or until she discovered he was a Freemason. Catherine ran him out of Imperial Russia.

Together he and Lorenza were run out of many cities and countries but always amassed another fortune. Typical of their M.O. is the arrival of the pair in Strasbourg in 1780. After taking a suite in the grandest hotel, they invited the richest people in the city to dinner. The Count did a few party tricks, which included the laying on of hands to cure aches and pains and the guessing of numbers written by guests on napkins. All this time, conversation ensued, during which Lorenza, who at the time was twenty-five, made reference to her twenty-eight-year-old son, a sea captain out of Holland. There were gasps of astonishment. Lorenza smiled cryptically when asked her age, and took from her bodice a bottle of the Count's elixir of life. It was the same dyed water that he had peddled as a young man long before he had the help of a beautiful wife.

But the Count began doing something strange. He would venture into the worst neighbourhoods and treat sick people without asking a fee. For most of the rest of his life, when he wasn't in prison, this would be the pattern: fleecing rich suckers, treating sick indigents.

In Bordeaux he started a school of medicine and philosophy, claiming to impart the wisdom of the ancients and cure all diseases. The streets outside his hotel were packed day and night with every sick person who could get there. The city had to mount a permanent military guard to keep order. When he couldn't, in fact, restore eyesight to every blind person and make every cripple walk, Cagliostro slipped them some of the money he had bilked from the others who were jamming his salons to find the secret of eternal life.

The Count had induced a sort of mass hysteria, as he had done at Strasbourg, and, as happened there, people woke up one morning filled with anger and embarrassment at being duped.

In Paris, he arranged séances where generals came to discuss war with Caesar and Alexander, and lawyers to confer with Cicero. Meanwhile his wife was talking the bally, so to speak, assuring the folks that her husband was perfectly capable of making himself invisible and of being two places at once.

The first long stretch of time that the Count did in jail was in the Bastille, where he was ensconced in the affair of Marie Antoinette's necklace. His role in the complex affair remains unclear. The plot involved stealing the Queen's necklace, replacing the invaluable jewels with fakes, and selling the real ones. Basically, he was accused of being the sorcerer who put all the other fine citizens, like Cardinal de Rohan, through their paces.

Cagliostro spent six months in the Bastille waiting to stand trial, after which he was released for lack of evidence. The speech he gave in his defense during the trial—a transcript of which still exists—is surely one of the most incredible orations in history. It reads as if a collaboration between Cicero and Don King.

The next couple of years were like a sad replay of the great times. The couple pulled off more cons in England and on the continent, but some time later Cagliostro was arrested by the Inquisition in Rome when he was initiating two men into the Egyptian Rite. They were spies. He was thrown into the dungeon in the Castel Sant'Angelo, and soon after sentenced to death.

So the great con man finally had his castle, and he tried to escape from it. When he was caught, Cagliostro was transferred to a cell at the very top of the castle which itself stands on a summit of sheer-sided rock walls. They had to hoist him up there in a basket. He wrote on the walls of his cell every day and dated his work. The last entry is March 6, 1795. The Paris newspapers reported his death on October 6, 1795.

There was such an uproar over the news stories, that Napoleon ordered an investigation into the death of the man who called himself Cagliostro.

As for the beautiful Lorenza Feliciano, she was allowed to repair to a nunnery, but not before she gave the Inquisition all the information it needed to put her husband away forever. §

# Marchesa Luisa Casati (1881–1957)

MARCHESA LUISA CASATI WITH GREYHOUNDS. GIOVANNI BOLDINI, 1908.

There is a cliché born of the cinema age and applied to extravagant lives. To wit: if you made a movie about him or her and stuck to the facts, no one would believe it. The personification of the cliché is Marchesa Luisa Casati. There have been many films about her or based upon her life; they've starred Vivien Leigh and Ingrid Bergman, among others. Each film has been a dismal disaster for the simple reason that no actress was capable of inhabiting her presence, and no one would believe the script anyway. A true-to-life ending to a biographical film about the woman would be particularly melodramatic.

One just does not see it coming, the way it ends.

It is London, mid-1950s. A tall old woman in a long black coat, shiny from wear, and a ragged, moth-eaten tatter of leopard skin wound around her neck. She wears a hat with a veil and is tottering along the pavement, lace-gloved hand on the elaborately carved handle of a walking stick. The face behind the veil is ghastly white, eyes made up to resemble those of a raccoon: the pupils are red. Tangles of vermilion hair stick out from under the hat. The old ruin looks like someone costumed to scare children.

Seeing a dustbin, she begins to poke about inside, finds a bit of red cloth, pins it to her coat and continues on her way. Stop her and inquire where she is bound, and the lady may reply, "To luncheon with Sir so-and-so or with Countess what's-her-name or back to my little room in Beaufort Gardens."

Today, she would be called a bag lady. On that day or any like it in the mid-1950s, she would have been called, by those who didn't know the truth, a nutty old biddy with delusions of former grandeur. To those who knew who she was, she would have been called the most represented woman in visual art and literature in the history of the world other than the Virgin Mary. It could also be said of her, in absolute truth, that "She used to be the richest woman in Europe and the most flamboyant woman in the world."

As a very young woman, Luisa Ammon decided to make her life a work of art. She certainly achieved her goal.

Her parents were Austrian and Italian. Her father made a vast fortune from cotton and, at nineteen, Luisa married the Marchese Camillo Casati. He got a beautiful young girl and a fortune. She got a title. To entertain herself while the husband was out hunting, Luisa began to study mysticism and the occult. A year after the marriage, she started to live a separate life, to dress unconventionally, associate with sorcerers and artists, and to have affairs. She had an affair with Gabriel D'Annunzio, the notorious poet, known as the "Prince of Decadence." He had conquered many women and would overwhelm many more. But Luisa Casati he would love for the rest of his life. D'Annunzio cared nothing for conventional notions of how a woman should behave, and he opened up a world of experience for Luisa. But he never dominated her as he did all his other women because she stood up to him, and defied him. She was so beautiful, he wrote, she impressed her image "on the air." Likewise, she "imprinted her face in my immortal substance."

It was not long after beginning her affair with the poet that Luisa's appearance began its drastic change.

No longer could she merely be called unconventional or extravagant; caring nothing for fashion, she stepped into another dimension.

She was continually on the move from her apartment in Milan to the one in Rome to the Ritz Hotel in Paris to her villa in Venice; each of these she decorated herself. She had constructed metal staircases and pink marble fountains. Wild animals roamed the grounds. The lady drove the staff and management crazy at the Ritz.

When not at one of these residences, she could be found in Bulgaria or Munich. It was as if the Marchesa was a traveling one-person theatre. But she was not an actress; her public appearances weren't scheduled in advance; she did not seek out audiences. One friend came upon her in America, alone, at the Grand Canyon. Her hair was red, her once-green eyes now red from daily drops of belladonna, her eyelashes two inches long, skin white, lips cinnabar. She wore high heel sandals and her feet were stained purple. She was dressed all in black with a feather headdress. Around her neck were miles of pearls as well as a necklace of tourist baubles, including Indian dolls and straw horses.

Sir Compton Mackenzie observing her step ashore on the Isle of Capri: "The Marchesa arrived on the Piazza from the funicular, escorted by an effeminate cicisbeo on whose arm one of her own rested. In her other arm was a gilded gazelle...presently an enormous Negro appeared, carrying a blue parrot in a cage."

The Marchesa invited the Scottish author for lunch. "I passed on to the salon and went in. Surprise scarcely expresses what I felt when I saw my hostess lying on the big black bearskin in front of the huge fireplace...lying there with absolutely nothing on."

Of lovers there were legions, including the founder of the Futurist movement in the arts, Filippo Marinetti, and painters Kees Van Dongen and Augustus John. There were dozens who painted, sculpted and photographed her, including Alberto Martini, Giovanni Boldini, Romaine Brooks, Leon Bakst, Federico Beltran y Masses, Jacob Epstein, Giacomo Balla, Adolph de Meyer and Man Ray. One portrait of her, by an unidentified painter, was used by the Marchesa in place of a passport photo. She got away with it, too.

A recently-divorced Luisa turned forty in 1920, the year fashion changed. She was no Gibson girl and wouldn't be. If anything, she dressed more outrageously, lived more wildly. She threw grand parties during which, if she wore anything, it was something designed not by the new star Coco Chanel, but Barkst or Paul Poiret. Luisa Casati is said to be the first woman to wear Poiret's hobble skirt and minaret robe. René Lalique and Georges Fouquet designed her jewellery.

In 1927, Luisa discovered that she was twenty-seven million dollars in debt. Her lawyers and accountants demanded she change her way of living. She would have none of that. It is incredible to think that by selling her homes, apartments and antiques, she was able to discharge the debt. This left her with a blank slate on which to inscribe more debts. By the mid-1930s, all her furniture and all the portraits of herself had been sold. At age sixty, the Marchesa moved to London where she lived in a series of rooms of decreasing size, and existed by selling or bartering the last of her jewellery. She searched the dustbins for scraps to pin to her threadbare coats and dresses, new cast-off materials to apply to the work of art that was herself.

This, then, is the woman you would have seen on the pavement in London in the mid-1950s. Perhaps she was going to tea with one aristocrat or another. This is where Quentin Crisp encountered her the year before her death. "She was spectacular. She possessed a presence one would never forget… She presented those who adored her with an image of something they could never be, a being somehow beyond criticism and convention."

Augustus John wrote that the Marchesa, when at the end, would like to have been "shot, stuffed and displayed in a glass case."

In 1995, the Art Gallery of Ontario premiered a one-woman show, *Infinite Variety: Portrait of a Muse,* based on the Marchesa's life. The gallery also owns the 1919 Augustus John portrait, voted by patrons as the most popular work in the permanent collection. In 1998, John Galliano's Spring and Summer couture collection for Christian Dior was dedicated to and inspired by Luisa Casati. Lavishly illustrated biographies of her have appeared in several languages. Undoubtedly there will be other books based on her life.

There will probably be another biographical film someday soon. But it, like the others, will surely not succeed. The presence of Marchesa Luisa Casati cannot be inhabited. It is as if she existed—exists—somewhere outside time, outside space. §

# Samuel Franklin Cody (1867–1913)

The greatest figure in the pioneer days of British aviation—a master kite builder, the first person to take to the air in a motorized vehicle, and the holder of all the early records—was an American cowboy, a genuine Texas sharpshooter, horse wrangler, cowpuncher and star of Wild West Shows: Samuel Franklin Cody, son of the great Buffalo Bill, later named Colonel Cody by King George.

The fellow made quite a spectacle of himself in turn-of-the-century England, on stage, on the streets, and in the air, usually attired in buckskin, boots, and a huge sombrero, moustache waxed, ready to spin a yarn of the cow trails and gambling dens in that fabled land west of the Mississippi. He'd bested Wyatt Earp at cards and Annie Oakley at trick shooting. Yes, Sam Cody had seen it all, including the horrendous deaths of his parents and his siblings, wiped out in an Indian raid on the family homestead near Birdville, Texas. Nine-year-old Cody, who hid in the woodpile after being wounded in the leg, somehow managed to drag himself the ten miles into Fort Worth and to a doctor.

Fortunately, truth is not the major determinant of a good story, or the man would have gotten the hook from the stage manager, banned from the campfire, and thrown through the swinging doors of the saloon. Nothing wrong with slinging the bull, but one must have a good grip on the animal.

SAMUEL FRANKLIN CODY, 1909. IMAGE COURTESY OF THE LIBRARY OF CONGRESS.

He was actually born Franklin Samuel Cowdery in Davenport, Iowa, in 1867. His father was not a hero in the Mexican and Civil Wars, but a lazy no-account. Franklin went to work when he was six, however, and claimed to have started riding before he started walking. That may have been true. He is listed in the 1880 Davenport City Directory as being a "horse trainer." He saddled up the next year and found work breaking horses in Montana. He was fourteen.

He was befriended by an older wrangler named Jake Ross, a well-known cowboy and horse breaker who later toured the west riding bulls and broncos at fairs. In his memoirs, Ross wrote that the kid was an even better rider than he was. "In fact, he was the best I ever saw."

By 1882, Cowdery had become a full-fledged cowboy on the newly established Long Drive from Texas to Montana. He was one of the infamous "hash-knife cowboys," named for the cattle brand in the form of the knife used to cut meat for hash. This was the group and this was the drive that is the origin of all the mythologizing of the wild life of the cowboy, the gun-toting saloon-wrecking icon of the Wild West.

There are two components to Cody's legacy; one is myth, and the other is skill and competence. He saw to the first, and the second was, evidently, inherent. A good cowboy was versatile, had to tend the animals and repair the equipment. Cody could build and repair anything.

Ross remembers Cody spending his spare time practicing "trick roping." When asked why he was doing that, Cody replied, "Well this way of life won't last long. I may go into show business."

He got into show business, but exactly how that happened is not known. His standard version of events seems as likely as any other. Cody said that circus manager Adam Forepaugh, having heard of his exploits, wired him to join his show at once. Exactly how Barnum's main rival heard of him, Cody never explained. What is true is that one day he was cowboying in Texas under the name of Frank Cowdery, and a few days later he was cowboying in Philadelphia under the name of California Frank. From the outset he thrilled Eastern audiences with his fancy riding and fancy shooting. Before too long he changed his handle to Captain Cody. It was the enterprising Forepaugh who realized that his young cowboy looked just like a younger version of Buffalo Bill, who happened to be the impresario's main rival. He encouraged his charge to grow his hair and his moustache and dress in buckskins. Forepaugh encouraged rumours that there was a family connection between his Captain and the old man.

Cody went from Forepaugh to join Annie Oakley in her production of *Deadwood Dick*. At season's end, Oakley found she hadn't turned a profit and went back to Buffalo Bill's show. Talk of an affair between Annie and Cody is questionable, for the simple reason that Annie usually preferred girls.

In Norristown, Pennsylvania in 1889, he married Maud Lee, a local girl, and soon incorporated her into his act with Forepaugh. Mainly what he did was shoot glass balls off Maud's head with a pistol. They were on the road for two years until Forepaugh succumbed to the flu and his heirs sold off the show. The Codys went to England, where the young man created a sensation in London in his flamboyant attire. He had posters printed advertising him and his wife as the son and daughter of Buffalo Bill Cody. Neither Sam nor the shows he was with realized that besides being a legend of the old west, Buffalo Bill was litigiously modern.

Perhaps troubles over the lawsuit broke up their marriage. No one knows. Soon enough though, Sam had another woman off whose head to shoot glass balls. She was Lela Davis, the daughter of a horse buyer. She was ten years older than Sam and the love of his life. He accepted her several children and incorporated them into his shows. They toured Europe, where Cody made good money on the side, racing on horseback against bicyclists. He remained in show business until 1901 but began experimenting with kites two years earlier. There is no record of him in England in 1898, so it may be true that he went to the Yukon in search of gold. Perhaps it is equally true that a Chinese cook in a Klondike camp taught him to fly a kite. Back in England, he spent his free time away from the theatre attempting to send and keep aloft bigger and bigger kites. He began to ascend in chairs fastened to those kites, such constructions being known as "man-lifting kites."

In 1901, he patented a two-cell box kite with wings. This is still called Cody's Bat Kite, considered by most kite aficionados to be the most beautiful kite ever made. In 1903, he crossed the English Channel in a canvas boat towed by a large bat kite. In 1905, riding one of his kites, Cody reached a height of 3,500 feet. Two years later, a Cody-designed kite carrying him and two passengers set the world record for staying aloft: three hours, twenty-five minutes.

Cody became a hero. Journalists and children followed him everywhere. He was the most daring adventurer in England, and a colourful character without peer. It wasn't long before he began to concentrate on powered flight and, in early 1908, was able to take off and stay in the air. On the sixteenth of October, 1908, Cody made the first officially recorded instance of powered flight in Great Britain. His aircraft, called *British Army Aeroplane No 1,* traveled 1,390 feet.

Cody had been under contract to the War Department to develop airplanes for the government, yet soon after he made his pioneer flight, his contract was cancelled. The Secretary of State for War declared there was no future for the use of aircraft.

So without army sponsorship, Cody had to raise his own money, build planes in rented sheds, and use farmers' fields for landing and taking off. In 1909, he became the first pilot to carry a passenger and made a world record flight of one hour and three minutes.

King George began to frequent Cody's flying exhibitions and the cowboy aviator got in the habit of landing his plane just a few feet from the monarch. Although he was criticized for this in the press, the King loved it and pronounced him Colonel Cody.

In the few years left to him, Cody took part in tests and challenges and won them more often than not. Unlike his famous fellow competitors—Delagrange, de Havilland, Sopwith, Bleriot, Santos-Dumont—he had no sponsorship. Cody and his family lived on the money he earned.

Cody also invented the seaplane. He was trying the new plane out on the seventh of August, 1913, a practice run for his planned attempt to cross the Atlantic Ocean. The plane broke in half over Laffan's Plain and Cody fell three hundred feet to his death.

Over 150,000 mourners showed up in Aldershot for the old cowboy's funeral.

For days the newspapers ran stories about him. Some of the journalists decided to research his background and found that Cody hadn't married Lela and, in fact, still had a wife in Pennsylvania. Maud had joined a trapeze act after splitting up with Cody and suffered a fall that caused her to be what was called "addle-brained." She was alert enough, however, to tell reporters, "Hell, his name wasn't Cody."

When it became known that the great hero was a man from Iowa named Cowdery, it didn't seem to matter a bit because by now it wasn't true. He had been Colonel Cody, and would be Colonel Cody, forever. Sam always did have a good grip on the bull. §

# Morris "Two-Gun" Cohen (1881–1970)

> "He was like something somebody wrote."
> —Emily Hahn, *The New Yorker*

I have a vision of a Chinese guy in Saskatoon or Edmonton, coming up to Morris Cohen in a backroom poker game and waving a Chinese newspaper in his face: "Morris! Morris! Here's the job you've been waiting for. You certainly have all the credentials."

WANTED: Aide de Camp to Sun Yat-sen. May lead to position as General in China. Applicant must have been born in Poland. Childhood spent hustling at Billingsgate Market and fighting in smokers. Reform-school education required. Farm labour, card tricks, and real estate fraud in Canada a must. Applicant must display ability to load dice and deal from bottom of deck, have lengthy arrest record, and have done time in prison. Oft-broken nose essential. Must be able to prove lifetime of knavery, chicanery and skullduggery. Jewish only need apply.

Novelist Saul Bellow once said he used to joke about Two-Gun Cohen, and indeed the guy sounds like a routine from the Yiddish theatre, but nobody joked about him to his face. He was what Jewish people called "a tough Jew." Probably the toughest of his time, and that was a long time.

He was born Abraham Miaczn in a *shtetl* in Poland in 1887. The family made it to London when Abraham was five years old, changed

COHEN ON HIS FIRST RETURN TO ENGLAND, 1911, AGE TWENTY-TWO.

their name to Cohen, and his to Morris. They lived in the East End, around the corner from where Jack the Ripper had recently murdered "Long Liz" Stride. Morris's first job, at age six, was working for a glazier as sort of an advance man, breaking windows. But mostly he stole. At nine, he was boxing, at ten, shilling for a thief known as Harry the Gonif. He graduated to picking pockets, was busted in 1900, and given five years in reform school.

Upon his release in 1905, Cohen was sent to Canada, a Barnardo boy, to a farm near Wapella, Saskatchewan. The hired hand turned out to be a card sharp and gunman, and taught Morris everything he knew.

After that apprenticeship, Morris drifted to Winnipeg to practice what he'd learned. He also became a pimp and got sent to prison for six months for being with an underage girl that he was "breaking in."

The first bend in the road that would eventually lead Cohen in a new direction occurred in a Saskatoon gambling den, at the back of a store owned by a Chinese man named Mah Sam. A guy came in one night and tried to rob the place. Even though the robber was armed, Cohen attacked him and beat him up. It must be understood that, at the time, even the idea of a white man coming to the aid of a Chinese man was just about unimaginable.

It turned out that Mah Sam was a supporter of Sun Yat-sen who at the time was trying to unite anti-Manchu factions to make a revolution in China.

A few weeks after the incident, Cohen was arrested for picking a pocket and given a year's hard labour in Prince Albert Penitentiary. A month later, Cohen was joined in prison by Mah Sam, sentenced to six months for running a gambling joint. The two became inseparable buddies. There being nothing the fifty-five-year-old Chinese man could teach the twenty-year-old Jewish kid about gambling, he schooled him in the politics of China.

After Cohen's release, and after February 12, 1912, when a Republican government was installed in China, he was taken to Calgary and voted into the Tongmenghui, after pledging to devote himself "to the service of Sun Yat-sen and the liberation of the Chinese people."

Cohen moved to Edmonton, sold real estate, and trained men to fight for Sun. He eventually became the liaison between the white press and the Chinese community. When war broke out, Cohen enlisted and sailed to England with his unit, but didn't join them in Belgium until five months later. He spent the time in hospital with gonorrhea.

After the war, Cohen worked for the Chinese Nationalist League, and was soon a political power, controlling the votes of all eight hundred Chinese in Edmonton.

On November 23, 1922, Cohen boarded a ship in Vancouver, bound for China. In his pocket he had a commission from Sun Yat-sen to facilitate a deal with a railway contractor. Cohen had a purpose to his life and eight weapons in his baggage.

After Cohen sold Sun on the railroad contract, he talked himself into a job, as adjutant or bodyguard. Not long after beginning his employ, Cohen was wounded in the left arm when an enemy fired at Sun. Cohen shot back and killed the would-be assassin. He later reasoned that if the bullet had struck his right arm, he would have been unable to reach his revolver and fire back. Thus he took to wearing a gun on each side, and a nickname was born.

Cohen dedicated himself to his leader, who made Cohen his confidante. After the death of Sun, Cohen drifted around China working as a factotum and fixer, and these would be his roles for most of the rest of his life. Following a trip around the world with exiled Chinese leaders, Cohen got into the arms business. He endeavoured to bring arms into China without going through the Russians. He was up to all sorts of shenanigans, even purchasing gunboats to fight pirates north of Hong Kong.

But besides the wheeling and dealing that some thought questionable at best, Cohen helped people—got them visas, or their relatives out of jail. He entertained lavishly, and his friends were of all nationalities and religions, all classes. He held court and hosted at the Astor House or David's Café in Kowloon. He was loud, full of himself and an indefatigable storyteller. Emily Hahn wrote, "It was sort of a hazard going through the lobby of the Peninsula Hotel; if you didn't run into General Cohen you were apt to fall in with One-arm Sutton."

When the Japanese seized Hong Kong in 1938, Cohen was taken into custody, beaten, and sent to the Stanley Prison Camp where he stayed until the Second World War was over.

In 1946, Cohen was in San Francisco for the first sessions of the new United Nations, in the role of liaison between Zionists and the government of China. He returned to China, but most of his deals didn't reach fruition. Cohen's problem was that he couldn't accept the new China. He sat around hotel lobbies trying to conjure the past out of his cigar smoke.

Cohen married in Montreal but it didn't last. He was always

traveling, spending prodigiously, and soon enough ran out of money. The big time hustler was reduced to putting his Chinese furniture into shops on consignment.

After his divorce, Cohen moved to England in 1951 and, at age sixty-four, seemed destined to live out his remaining days as a garrulous old bore who used to be somebody important. Then, a few years later, his life changed. This late phase might be called The Hustler Reborn. Cohen was hired by Rolls-Royce as a "consultant" to the China market, a go-between, actually, who would grease the wheels and grease the palms to sell motors and planes.

So the fixer and the schmoozer was back, a fixture again in China's hotel lobbies. After years of declaring Mao's regime an aberration that wouldn't last, he became a steadfast supporter.

The Rolls-Royce deal lasted for several years but Cohen had other irons in other fires. One lucrative score was a sinecure with the Archives of the Revolution, jotting down the stories he'd been giving away for decades. On one of his rare trips to North America, he appeared as a guest on the CBC television show *Front Page Challenge*.

Back in China, when he wasn't making his rounds, Cohen was to be found in the lobby of the old Beijing Hotel, a living museum piece, seemingly the embodiment of exactly what the Revolution opposed: a broken-nosed old individualist adventurer in a Bond Street suit, swinging his Malacca-headed cane and spinning yarns.

A lot of western journalists thought Cohen was full of it, a big blowhard, but big business and the Chinese still had a use for him. In 1962, he got a job with Decca Radar Ltd., to sell equipment, and in 1966, at age seventy-nine, Cohen was in Beijing brokering deals for Canadian and Argentine wheat to be brought into the country.

He returned to England in 1967 and his health immediately began to decline. Cohen spent his last couple of years smoking cigars, telling the old tales, and distributing the last of his money to kids on the street. His funeral, in September, 1970, was a traffic stopper. It took the death of a two-gun-toting Jewish jailbird and card sharp to bring officials from Communist China and Taiwan together in public for the first time. §

# Arthur Cravan (1887–?)

*Salina Cruz, Oaxaca, Mexico*—I'm down on the waterfront of this large, gritty, southern city that sprawls along the Pacific Ocean. The Navy is here, oil refineries and mammoth tankers from all over the world, and a vast fishing fleet. Only at this particular section of the docks can I begin to conjure up what it might have been like back in 1918. There are still a couple of old hotels with wrought-iron balconies, courtyards with crumbling cement fountains, and saloons where tough men knock back pulque and hookers watch the swinging doors to show them the next john. These are not the kinds of establishments where the hombres at the bar make way for a gringo. But they would have edged sideways for Arthur Cravan, and if any one of them looked at Mina Loy the wrong way, well, it wouldn't have happened again, *señor*.

Leave the hotel, turn left, and cross the road to the wharf where a few small boats used to tie up. Just over there is where Cravan worked on the boat he bought after he climbed out of his sickbed and beat the Mexican heavyweight champion in twelve rounds. In 1918, there was à big tree where the tackle shop is now, and Mina Loy sat in the shade, writing poetry and watching Arthur work. When the boat was ready, Cravan took it out for a tryout sail.

Early in his boxing career, Cravan would shout out his accomplishments before the bell for the first round. He claimed to be "jewel

A YOUNG ARTHUR CRAVAN. NO ATTRIBUTION.

thief, smuggler, pimp, poet with the world's shortest haircut, nephew of Oscar Wilde . . ." Of all his boasts, the claim to a connection with the infamous Wilde was the one that caused the most offence, but it is the one most easily proved.

Cravan was born Fabian Avernius Lloyd in Lausanne, Switzerland. His mother was Wilde's sister, the family having fled Britain at the height of the Wilde-Douglas scandal. That Douglas's father was the Marquis of Queensbury, who laid down the rules for modern prizefighting, is just one of the ironies of Cravan's life.

Cravan's formal education was acquired at private schools throughout Europe. He was thrown out of several. In his teens he began to take an interest in prizefighting, but was too restless to pursue the sport seriously. As soon as he finished school, the young man began frequenting the *demimonde* of European cities, particularly Paris and Berlin. He was big and handsome and women adored him. Somewhere around this time, he began calling himself Arthur Cravan. He dabbled in boxing and hustling, and shipped out to Australia to avoid the police.

For several years he knocked around the world, working in gold mines in New Guinea and California and in the oilfields of Venezuela. He is rumoured to have been a pimp in Melbourne. Back in Paris in 1906, he won the French amateur light heavyweight championship, and turned professional.

The decade and a half from the turn of the last century to the declaration of war in 1914 is considered to have seen the greatest explosion of cultural activity since the Renaissance. Art cast off the stifling cloak of musty convention and modernism was revealed. No longer were certain subjects considered too vulgar for art. Cravan began to write poetry that took the whole world as its theme and celebrated the excitement and dynamism of the new age.

He started a magazine called *Maintenant* that represented a one-man assault on bourgeois values. In its pages, Cravan exposed phonies and false gods, subjecting them to sarcasm and ridicule. When one painter protested Cravan's critique of his work, the boxer-poet replied that in retaliation he would have sex with the man's wife, after which she would not be content with normal men.

Cravan used a wheelbarrow to distribute *Maintenant* throughout Paris. One issue was devoted to skewering painters who had contributed to the annual Salon. Seven of the offended jumped Cravan while he was making his rounds. He sent six of them to hospital and the seventh ran away.

Despite his size—six feet five, two hundred thirty pounds—and his history as a fighter and roustabout, Cravan was said to not have a mean bone in his body. It did not, therefore, surprise his close friends that when war was declared, Cravan, now known as "The Great Arthur" and "The Colossus," refused to have anything to do with what he considered mass murder sanctioned by abhorrent criminals.

He took off for Portugal with artists Robert Delaunay and Francis Picabia. By 1916, he was in Spain, where he ran into his old friend Jack Johnson, the first black heavyweight champion. Johnson had been stripped of his title because of a trumped-up morals charge and was as broke as Cravan. One night in a Barcelona barroom, they came up with the idea of fighting each other. News of the bout created such a sensation that the huge bullfight arena had to be rented to accommodate the crowd.

On fight night, the arena was packed with excited fans. Johnson was world famous, of course, but Cravan had become a sensation because of his flamboyant life in the wild port city. Fully confident of being knocked out in the first round, Cravan found himself actually leading on points by the fifth. The only problem was that he had booked passage on a freighter bound for New York that very night. In the sixth round, a desperate Arthur went, in the vernacular of the fight game, into the tank. As soon as the referee had counted ten over him, Cravan jumped up and headed for the docks, reaching the ship just as its whistle was blowing. During the crossing, Cravan was befriended by a disillusioned revolutionary, fleeing the Soviet Union under an assumed name. He's remembered as Leon Trotsky.

In New York, Cravan fell in with avant-garde artists, many of them from Europe, who were just beginning to call themselves Dadaists. He was a man whose life, whose desires, whose expression knew no boundaries. He didn't have a place to live. He slept in the rooms of willing women and, on odd nights when he was alone, curled up on a bench in Central Park.

And then he met Mina Loy.

If Cravan was considered the epitome of masculinity, Mina Loy, poet and painter, was his female counterpart. She was Goddess to his Colossus, and the first time they met, they hated each other. To Mina, he was a swaggering braggart; Arthur thought she was a frigid, solipsistic prude.

At their second meeting, they fell hopelessly in love. While Arthur was notorious as a womanizer, Mina was equally renowned for being untouchable. Marcel Duchamp is said to have offered generous odds that Mina and Arthur would never get together, but could find no takers. And they did get together—on the night Mina bailed Arthur out of the Riker's Island jail.

They became inseparable, exploring New York, going to the theatre, making love. At least, they were inseparable until the United States entered the war, and Cravan had to take off for Canada. It is known that he hitchhiked to Montreal. A month later, he was in Newfoundland, working on fishing boats on the Grand Banks. For several months there was no word from Cravan; then he showed up in Mexico City, proprietor of a boxing academy.

By the time Mina Loy joined him, the academy had burned down and Cravan was making a living as a professional fighter. Previously he had dabbled at the sport, impressing mainly naïve artistic types; now he was fighting for real, before hostile crowds in towns like Monterrey and Guadalajara. After beating the Mexican champion, Cravan relocated with Loy to Salina Cruz and stayed at a hotel run by a German deserter and anarchist. While he worked on the boat, Mina, six months pregnant with their child, waited on shore, writing poetry and drawing. Finally, the day arrived when Cravan considered his labours complete. He decided to try the boat out on a sail around local waters. Mina waved as he moved away from shore.

I'm standing right there now, the same place Mina stood, eighty-two years ago, looking west at sunlight glittering on blue water.

She never saw him again.

Three months after Cravan disappeared, she had their baby, a daughter she named Fabienne. While the little girl was still an infant, Mina Loy began her search for her husband. Loy claimed to have stopped at every prison in Mexico, Central and South America, her baby in her arms. She refused to believe Cravan had drowned. He had to be alive, but unable to contact her.

Loy spent the '20s running a boutique in Paris, but, by the beginning of the next decade, it was clear to her family and friends that she was becoming increasingly disoriented. By the 1940s, Loy was living in cheap rooming houses in New York City. A well-known street character, she dragged trash and junk back to her room to be used in collages and assemblages. In 1960, Loy's daughter and son-in-law took her to Vail, Colorado, where she lived above a tea shop and became known as a crazy recluse who claimed to have once led an exciting life.

As for Cravan, there are those who insist that he did not die at sea, that he became an art forger, a hero of the French resistance, the owner of vast estates in Chile; one scholar has even "proven" that Cravan surfaced in Mexico as the German anarchist novelist known as B. Traven.

Mina Loy died in 1966. A magazine interviewer once asked her what was the happiest moment of her life. "Every moment," she replied, "that I spent with Arthur Cravan." §

# Charles Cros (1842–1888)

It was a summer morning in 1881 in the Batignolles section of Paris, and the previous night's dinner party was finally winding down. At four in the morning, the poet and inventor, absinthe abuser, and all around ragamuffin Charles Cros—he had thick curly black hair and a broad nose and has been described as resembling a Pacific Islander—stood, cleared his throat and extemporaneously bespoke an artistic revolution.

What Cros recited had a title, "The Kippered Herring," but there was no name for whatever it was, for whatever it was had no precedent. But typical of Cros, it wasn't new for him. He had a suitcase full of things just like it. They were sort of mini-plays, combining poetry, diatribe, and jokes.

Within a few days, however, these works by Cros had been christened. The actor Ernest Coquelin was at the Batignolles dinner, and when Cros spoke, he'd heard not only innovation but fortune. Coquelin bought the contents of Cros's suitcase and began to recite it to paying audiences. He called the works "monologues."

Thus, Cros, who had already published the first plans for colour photography and would later do the same for the phonograph, was the inventor of both stand-up comedy, of the Lord Buckley-Lenny Bruce variety, as well as performance art.

Soon Cros was expanding the scope of his pieces, setting them to

CHARLES CROS: (1842–1888) POET AND INVENTOR OF THE PHONOGRAPH. PHOTO BY NADAR IN 1879. © CORBIS/BETTMANN.

music and performing them, often with Coquelin. This was not the birth of the art-song but the creation of the radical art song. Bob Dylan, Joni Mitchell, Tom Waits, not to mention generations of French singers like Jacques Brel, Charles Trenier, and Juliette Greco—they are all there in Charles Cros.

Before he died, much too early, in 1888, he would also invent the forerunner of what came to be known as rap music. But we'll get to that.

The genius was born in the Pyrenees in 1842. His first job was teaching at a sanatorium for deaf mutes. His free time was devoted to studying medicine and writing poetry. Cros came to Paris in 1865, with the notion of building a telegraph line to Peru. This didn't work out, but two years later he was at the World's Fair demonstrating his revolutionary automatic telegraph. Cros then began to study colour photography, and in 1869 produced a study that explained how colour pictures could be created. Cros's photograph of his friend Manet's painting "Spring" is the first successful colour picture ever taken. It would be five months before the similar ideas of Louis Ducos du Hauron were published; nevertheless, it is du Hauron who is generally credited with being the inventor of colour photography and not Cros.

Cros has been called the best poet of his time—"his time" meaning immediately pre-Rimbaud. Incidentally, when Rimbaud stepped off the train from Charleville he was met by Charles Cros, whose poetry influenced the young, soon-to-be guttersnipe. Later, the two men had a falling out—not when Rimbaud seduced Verlaine, but when he seduced Verlaine's wife; Verlaine's wife's brother, Charles de Sivry, was Cros's best friend.

Cros's first book, however, was not poetry but a work entitled, *Studies on the means of Communication with the Planets*. Cros envisioned focusing electric lights on a huge concave mirror that would send the flashing equivalent of Morse code to Mars or Venus.

In the 1870s, Cros, along with comedian Alphonse Allais, organized a group of artists who called themselves Hydropathes, which is translated either as Water-Haters or Water-Curers, although the first meaning is probably more appropriate given that all participants, and they included caricaturist André Gill and poet Jules Laforgue, dedicated themselves to getting drunk, as well as to writing poetry and satirizing bourgeois society.

In 1881, a failed painter named Rodolphe Salis had the idea to found a nightclub that would cater to artists and others who were against the dull and stifling culture of the dominant society. He called it Le Chat Noir, and it was a sort of super salon, featuring poetry readings, monologues, plays and anarchist speeches on three floors. There was even a Le Chat Noir newspaper and literary review. Salis was the host and he initiated the habit of insulting his guests—or, at least, some of them; The Black Cat was wildly successful and attracted the slumming bourgeoisie. Salis dissed them and meant it, and they loved it.

The Black Cat may have presented anti-establishment comedians but it was in dead earnest. The place was in constant artistic upheaval, and there has probably never been anything like it, though imitations began to arise immediately, most notably Le Mirliton of Aristide Bruant, the man with the black hat and red scarf in the poster by Toulouse Lautrec. Soon there were Black Cats all over the world, but it is probably impossible to realize now what the original was like, simply because it is probably impossible to imagine an authentic radical artistic culture. It was pure bohemia, which by definition included all levels of society. Unlike latter-day debased bohemia, the Black Cat culture was not a sort of minor league of the establishment, filled with temporary anarchists waiting to move up. What's more, clubs and cafes, bistros and bars like the Black Cat were able to support their artists. All the people from that era whom we remember were of that milieu.

And probably the best of that milieu, the most truly original, was Charles Cros. Kenneth Rexroth has called him "... the most important poet-singer of mid-century Paris, and his poems spoke of a way of life completely unassimilable by the hypocritical, debauched and puritanical society of Louis Napoleon's gimcrack Second Empire."

On April 30, 1877, Charles Cros sent a registered package to the

Secretary of the Academy of Sciences. Inside the package was a paper, "Process of Reproducing Audible Phenomena." This was the first such process. Cros was a poor poet and did not have the money to make a working model, which was required to get a patent for his "parleophone." Thomas Edison had money for a working model, and thus, in December, eight months after Cros's plans were filed, Edison was given the first patent for a phonograph. But Edison's machine was a crude device, a stylus playing upon a vertical tin foil cylinder. The machine stopped working when the tin foil wore out. Cros' parleophone was a disc-based system that not only recorded but played back sounds; this is the system still used in records, picking up sounds in grooves on a disc. This method was manufactured in 1887 by Emile Berliner and called the gramophone.

The final irony: in 1888, six months after the gramophone appeared on the market and six months before the greatest artist-scientist since Leonardo da Vinci died, Charles Cros went into a recording studio and made a record reading his poetry to music. One side, "With Flowers and With Women," is his ode to absinthe. The poem and the recording probably earned Cros his entry into the Absinthe Hall of Fame. The curators of that august body, in further recognition of his prodigious appetite for "the green fairy," call Cros "the original twenty a day man." The performance could be considered probably the first rap record ever made. The other side, "The Smoked Herring," is even more remarkable, a pre-dada thumbing of the nose at the pretensions of adults and other dullards. Cros recites the lines, sings them and even provides commentary on them, very much like Shaggy does one hundred and more years later.

Cros was a genius, the comparison with da Vinci not far-fetched at all. But Cros had neither a Sforza or Francis I behind him. His only faithful companion was absinthe, and it killed him at the age of forty-six. §

# Lady Jane Digby (1807–1881)

IMAGE: PAINTING BY JOSEF STIELER.

The lady, and she was a Lady, certainly got the funeral she deserved. And, like so many episodes in her life, it took an unpredictable twist.

The ceremony began respectably enough on that Damascus day in 1881, just as her life had begun conventionally seventy-four years earlier in England—very solemn, very Anglican. Men and women with somber expressions and clothes to match, trudging along in a cortege that wound through the colourful bazaar like a turgid black snake.

Suddenly, the carriage of the chief mourner flew open. The deceased's husband leaped out with a cry of frustration and ran off in the opposite direction. "Well, what might one expect?" no doubt issued from more than one pair of pursed lips.

The cortege had reached the Christian cemetery and the coffin was being lowered into the ground when the husband reappeared, mounted on his wife's favourite Arabian stallion. He stared into the grave for several minutes, then turned the horse and galloped away toward the desert.

He was a Bedouin sheik, king of his people, Medjuel el Mezrab. Thus, his wife, who had begun as a lady, ended as a queen. In between she had been a baroness, a countess, a princess. One chronicler of Jane Digby's life wrote that she "tossed away titles like confetti."

Medjuel was Jane Digby's fourth husband (or tenth, if one believes the rumours about six Italians during several undocumented years) and there were innumerable lovers, but she was not an adventuress like Lola Montez. Jane Digby didn't use outrageous charms to entice men and, once they had fallen hopelessly, take them for whatever she wished—mansion, title, jewellery, a ticket on the next coach to Italy. No, Lady Jane was mad for love, to love and be loved, and when she didn't and wasn't, she filled the spaces with desperate erotic encounters. This woman who started out experimenting with a stable boy at age thirteen would, at age seventy-three, complain to her diary that an entire month had passed since her husband had slept with her.

In 1816, Jane Digby was nine years old. That same year, Lord Byron fled England because of the scandal over his love affair with his half-sister. In exile, he became a legend, the romantic, the tortured hero, ready to give up anything for freedom. Byron made an impression on Jane even then, and after she left her first husband she sought men like Byron her entire life, and often found them.

The problem was she was a *woman* like Byron.

Maybe she thought her first husband was that kind of man. Lord Ellenborough was tall and handsome and known in the House of Lords for his sharp tongue. He wore the romantic aura of the widower, his wife having died in childbirth. His mother was constantly after him to remarry; his career demanded it. Ellenborough, consequently, proposed to the star of the 1825 season, sixteen-year-old Jane Digby.

Whatever happened on the honeymoon, it was a disaster. And the marriage wasn't any better. Lord Ellenborough devoted himself to his work, and it wasn't long before his young wife began going out on the town. One Wednesday night in April, 1826, Lord Ellenborough escorted Jane to a ball, left her, and went to a business meeting. Within an hour, Jane had met the love of her life thus far, and the romantic hero of all her fantasies: Prince Felix von Schwarzenberg, attaché to the

Hapsburg Empire and future Prime Minister of Austria. He was a dashing, dark-eyed adventurer, rumoured to have broken hearts in all his postings: Lisbon, St. Petersburg, Rio de Janiero.

Shortly after meeting von Schwarzenberg, Jane posed for a portrait by James Holmes, who had painted Byron and was a favourite of George IV. Anything anyone wants to know about Jane Dibgy's attraction is captured in that painting. She is wearing a laced bodice, leaning against a divan, shoulders mostly bare, eyes large and inviting, lips a bee sting. One has to believe the letter she's holding is from her lover—he has suggested a rendezvous, and she is musing on what may transpire.

What transpired with the Prince was a wild affair that created a scandal, led to a shocking divorce trial, bore Jane two children and, eventually, broke her heart.

True to the cliché of the cuckolded husband, Lord Ellenborough was the last to know, or pretended to be. He sued for divorce on grounds of adultery. Witnesses were procured who reported hearing Jane's cries of passion in various hotels. A newspaper cartoon depicted von Schwarzenberg attending to the stays of his mistress's corset. Lord Ellenborough was granted his divorce and Jane left England, never to return.

She went to Paris and briefly resumed the affair, but Prince Felix's superiors gave him an ultimatum: his career or the blonde. He chose the former, but he chose also to keep Jane dangling for years. He would write to her, professing his love and announcing his arrival. But he never showed up.

In the meantime, Jane was dabbling with Ludwig, King of Bavaria, and being courted by Baron Karl von Venningen. Honore de Balzac also was smitten, and used Jane as a character in several novels. "The peaches and cream woman," as he described her, "this creature who glows with a strange phosphorescence, had a constitution of iron."

Jane had a child by von Venningen, whom she had married one years earlier. She would pay as much attention to this child as she had to her others: next to none. The Baron was the most honourable of men, but honour wasn't enough for a woman who lived for passion. When von Venningen discovered Jane's affair with Count Spyridon Theotoky, he challenged the lover to a duel. The Baron almost killed the Count, but, paragon that he was, Venningen took Theotoky to his estate to be nursed. Several weeks later, when the Count was well enough to travel, he was off, taking the Baroness with him.

They went to Paris and then to Greece, where Theotoky was to manage his family's estates on Corfu. There Jane gave birth to a boy whom they named Leonidas and who died in 1846 in a fall from a balcony. His mother, who saw him plunge to the marble floor, later declared that Leonidas, the first of her children she had loved, had been taken from her as punishment for her neglect of the others.

After the son's death, Jane vanished. There was no trace of her for three years, until she appeared in Athens in 1849. In 1852, she commenced an affair with Cristos Hadji-Petros, a bandit hero known as the King of the Mountains. Once a local governor under the Turks, he had turned against the Ottoman Empire when the war of independence began in 1821. For several months, Jane gloried in the life of the mountains, going on raiding parties with the bandit and his brigands. The men were amazed that she rode as well as any of them.

The romance lasted only a few months, until Jane discovered that Hadji-Petros, then over sixty, was conducting affairs with two other women. Humiliated, Jane left Greece, ostensibly to visit Palmyra and buy Arab horses. A month after leaving Athens, near a Bedouin camp along the Jordan River, she entered a tent to negotiate the purchase of a stallion. Inside, she met a man named Saleh, twenty years her junior, and she was in love again.

They had a month together, but she was determined to complete her trip to Palmyra, outside the territory of Saleh's people. She was escorted across the desert by Mezrabs, whose leader was called Medjuel, and he, too, fell in love with Jane Digby.

But Jane was in love with the boy Saleh and returned to his camp on the Jordan—to find he had married a girl still in her early teens. Returning to Damascus, Jane wrote in her dairy, "If I had neither mirror nor memory, I would believe myself fifteen years old."

Evidently to prove her feelings predominated over her mirror, Jane conducted an affair with yet another Bedouin sheik after her caravan left Baghdad. This liaison ended when Jane berated the man for beating a camel.

Finally reaching Damascus, she found Medjuel waiting for her, vowing undying love, promising even to give up his other wives. After several weeks, Jane accepted him as she had accepted von Venningen. But there was a difference: she grew to love Medjuel.

They were together until she died. Part of each year they shared a house in Damascus, spending the rest of their time in the desert. Jane rode with the tribe, adopted their customs and dress. She became a legend, and, in Damascus, an early tourist attraction. Western visitors felt they had to have a glimpse of the famous swashbuckling courtesan. If scores of diaries are to be believed, none who had that glimpse was disappointed.

For two years during Jane's time in Syria, the equally fabled Captain Sir Richard Francis Burton was British Consul. Both were linguists, artists, and equestrians, with an interest in what were called antiquities, and they often rode together in the desert.

Burton, who knew a thing or two about life and women, said this of Jane Digby: "With her, life's poetry never sank to prose." §

# Florence Lowe "Pancho" Barnes (1901–1975)

Near the beginning of Philip Kaufman's film *The Right Stuff*, Sam Shepard, playing test pilot Chuck Yeager, walks into a weather-beaten California desert bar one particular night and begins to dance with his wife, the glamorous Glennis (Barbara Hershey). Then they go for a wild horseback ride through the desert. Most of this is true, except that the woman Yeager rode with was Pancho Barnes, the owner of the bar. And she wasn't glamorous.

The grease-stained, cigar-chomping dame whom Yeager and the other pilots knew as Pancho Barnes was officially named Florence Leontine Lowe at birth. But get past that, and the stories start to roll. There's the one about Pancho picking up Edgar Bergen at an airstrip, in a new Cadillac Eldorado filled with chickens. She'd bought both along the way—the car and the chickens.

Then there was the time that Pancho, aged sixty, decked her fourth husband (or was he the fifth? Anyway, he was half her age) with a right to the jaw. And who could forget when she belted Ramon Novarro after the handsome movie star told Pancho he couldn't sleep with her because, despite those torrid scenes with Garbo in *Mata Hari*, he was inclined toward boys? How about the time she took the woman's air speed record away from Amelia Earhart? Or when she shipped out on a freighter to Mexico dressed as a man?

Well, there are a million stories, because Florence Lowe Barnes

PHOTO COURTESY OF PANCHO BARNES ENTERPRISES, INC. USED WITH PERMISSION.

was, as the man who provided her nickname—a roustabout called Roger Chute—succinctly put it, "a social phenomenon and a goddamned force of nature."

She was born to wealth and privilege in July, 1901, and grew up in a forty-room mansion in San Marino, California. She spent her girlhood shunted from one private boarding school to the next, her family's way of dealing with the fact that Florence wasn't like other little girls; she was too rough, too adventurous, and cared little for the rules. She cared mainly for horses and other animals. Her parents' attempts to keep Florence on destiny's dull, affluent path was not helped by Professor Thaddeus Lowe, the little girl's maternal grandfather. If you want to stifle a little girl's dreams, convince her adventure is not ladylike, and that she ought to perfect her embroidery and housekeeping, then you had better keep any grandfather like Thaddeus far away from the kid.

Granddad Lowe had begun experimenting with balloons in his childhood in the 1830s, ran away from home to join a traveling medicine show, organized balloon flights over Confederate lines in the Civil War, was the first person to bomb an enemy from the air, was an inventor and flamboyant entrepreneur and, on January 16, 1910, took his granddaughter to the first aviation exhibition in America. After which, the old man told the little girl, "When you grow up, everybody will be flying."

Florence's life may be said to have been dominated by two obsessions. Flight was the first. The other got off to a less auspicious start. At age eighteen, in a sexual fever, she married the only suitor who met the approval of her parents, a young minister named C. Rankin Barnes. Their first physical encounter didn't take place until the fourth night of the honeymoon and lasted less time than Reverend Barnes's subsequent statement that he didn't like sex and had no interest in ever trying it again. Florence, however, *was* interested in trying it again with someone else, and with a lot of someones.

She fell in with a roaring '20s college crowd. Living apart from her husband, her young son Billy turned over to a nanny, she made her mansion a party house. One of the regular revelers was a USC football player named Marion Morrison, usually escorted by Duke, his German shepherd.

After a South American trip and a shipboard affair with an oilman, Florence shipped out of San Pedro on a freighter bound for Mexico. No sooner had they cleared port than it was revealed the ship was taking a supply of arms to a group of would-be revolutionaries. When the boat was seized off San Blas, Florence and Roger Chute jumped overboard, swam ashore and began a six-month overland adventure. At one point Chute, on horseback, said to Florence, who was then mounted on a burro, "You remind me of Pancho in *Don Quixote*."

"You mean Sancho Panza."

"Well, maybe so, but from now on I'm going to call you Pancho."

Back home she got work in the movies as a stuntwoman, doubling for Louise Fazenda in horseback riding scenes in the early Rin Tin Tin movies. Thrilled by the stunt fliers, Pancho got her pilot's license, and, when she wasn't flying in movies for Howard Hawks or Howard Hughes, went barnstorming and racing.

In August 1930, the women's air speed record (held by Amelia Earhart) was 184.6 miles per hour. On the fourth of that month, Pancho took the record, flying a Travel Air Model R at 196.19 miles per hour. Ensuing publicity encouraged her to organize a touring show dubbed the Pancho Barnes Flying Mystery Circus of the Air.

In 1933, Pancho bought a quarter section ranch in the Mojave desert. Her next-door neighbour was the newly arrived Army Air Corps, living in tents and setting up a bombing and gunnery range. Pancho's spread grew up alongside what would become Edwards Air Force Base. Soon she expanded her place to 368 acres that included, besides ranching operations, a landing strip and hangars. She added a swimming pool, bar, and guest cottages, and named her operation the Rancho Oro Verde Fly-Inn Dude Ranch. She managed to survive the Depression and thrive during the war and post-war boom. Pancho's Fly-Inn provided a place where servicemen could mingle with high society, desert rats and Hollywood personalities, a far more luxurious and interesting establishment than the pile of boards held up by cacti that Sam Shepard walks into in *The Right Stuff*. And Pancho was a lot rougher and tougher than Kim Stanley, who played her. "The only argument about her," Yeager said, "was whether she was the ugliest woman we had ever seen or just one of the ugliest." (To be fair, Yeager admired her enormously, and wrote "She was my friend.")

In the early 1950s, there was a change of guard at the air base, and the new straitlaced regime had no use for the likes of Pancho Barnes and her swashbuckling attitudes. Her place was declared off limits by the Air Force; then they seized her property, saying it was needed for a new runway. Pancho took the Air Force to court. The suits lasted for years. At one point, a fire destroyed many of the buildings on her property. The fire was judged to be arson, but the responsible party was never found. Pancho's considerable fortune was gone long before she lost the final suit.

By the beginning of the 1960s, she was living in a dirt-floor hovel even farther out in the desert. She developed breast cancer and had one breast, then the other, removed. But she beat the disease and took to wearing rubber breasts when she felt she had to maintain appearances. When an infrequent visitor knocked on her door, he—there weren't any shes—was usually greeted by Pancho's gruff voice calling, "Just a minute, 'til I strap on my tits."

She was tracked down in the middle 1960s by an aviation history buff who arranged for Pancho to move into a shack with running water on the outskirts of a town named Boron. Pancho had a half-acre lot that she filled with dogs, horses, cats and goats. Her idea had been to sell the animals, but she couldn't part with any.

During the last five years of her life, Pancho became sought after as a speaker at aviation functions. She would be brought out to enliven the proceedings with wild anecdotes about the rough-and-ready, seat-of-the-pants, good old days.

Which leads me to my favourite Pancho Barnes story. It happened around 1970, when a friend in the movie business took Pancho to the commissary at Universal Pictures. She was enjoying her free meal when a big man came up and put his hand on her shoulder. "Pancho," he said, "you remember me?"

"Yeah, you used to come to my parties way back. You're Marion Morrison."

But they didn't call him Marion any more. Thrusting out his chest, the man said, "I'm more than that now. I'm John Wayne."

Pancho looked John Wayne up and down and then turned back to her plate. "Big fucking deal," she said. "Now let me finish my meal." §

# Baroness Elsa von Freytag-Loringhoven (1874–1927)

Upon the Baroness, a famous poet declared, "the principle of non-acquiescence laid a burden." Put another way, she had no truck with compromise. She was *too much* and too hot to handle—though she encouraged many a man to try.

Here is a description of her sauntering forth on the streets of New York: "her hair shaved off and her scalp dyed purple, wearing an inverted coal scuttle for a hat, a vegetable grater as a brooch, long ice-cream spoons for earrings, and metal teaballs attached to her pendulant breasts . . ."

Just another punkette off for some bald-head banging, one might assume, or a member of Andy Warhol's entourage hanging about a film shoot, desperate to be noticed. Only the description of Baroness Elsa von Freytag-Loringhoven, the former Elsa Hildegard Plötz, dates from 1914, and that was just her everyday sauntering outfit.

Although born in Germany, she had hit Manhattan in 1913, via a pig farm in Kentucky. Immediately she made the scene, and bohemia reeled. Djuna Barnes, William Carlos Williams and the rest of them just didn't know what to make of her. The next year, Dada arrived from Europe, one step ahead of conscription, and found Elsa waiting for it. Duchamp, Picabia and the rest regarded her like newly arrived

IMAGE COURTESY OF THE LIBRARY OF CONGRESS.

anthropologists. Yet she was the personification of the cultural and societal nihilism they had made a movement about. Finally, not knowing what to do with her, they condescended, they memoir-ised her—and then they dropped her. But, Ezra Pound, who remarked upon her "non-acquiesence," did so in contrast to "the immense cowardice of advertised literati."

She was born in 1881 in a small town on the Polish-German border. Her father, a stone mason, beat and sexually abused her. At fifteen, Elsa left home and became an artist's model in Munich. In 1901, she married August Endell, an architect who turned out to be impotent. The next year, after numerous affairs, she hooked up with one Felix Paul Greve who would eventually change his name, invent a new biography for himself and become the well-known, if overrated, novelist of the Canadian prairie called Frederick Philip Grove. Greve was the first person, she later wrote, who gave her an orgasm.

In 1903, Elsa left with Greve and Endell on a trip to Sicily. While they were in Rome, Greve was arrested for fraud, and later convicted and sent to prison for a year. During his incarceration, Elsa resumed her promiscuous ways. In an unpublished autobiography, she is quite frank about her adventures, writing in a style totally free of artifice but replete with scatological detail as well as acute psychological awareness.

After his release, Greve and Elsa wandered around Europe. He worked as a translator and she as an artist's model and part-time prostitute. In 1905, Greve published some poems under the pseudonym Fanny Essler, which was the title of his first novel, based on the early life of Elsa Hildegard Plotz. Greve, who never let truth impinge on his own life story, was strictly accurate in his account of Elsa's.

In 1909, Greve, in trouble again—probably for stealing from the novelist Andre Gide—left for America, and Elsa followed shortly after. She found him on a pig farm in Kentucky. She must, at first, have thought he was hiding out or had lost his mind. Elsa, as unlikely as it may seem, tried, for a few weeks anyway, to be a pig farmer's wife. But she was not going to be the wife of a violent pig farmer who reminded her of her father, and she left.

After several months in places like Cincinnati, Cleveland, and Chicago, she reached New York and something that looked very much like freedom. Elsa began to write, make art, and dress as she pleased. She no longer had to defer to the phlegmatic prose of her husband, her assemblages were better than the works of the artists for whom she posed, and the most outrageously turned-out bohemians were so many prim librarians in comparison.

The future novelist Djuna Barnes caught her on the street in Greenwich Village in 1916: "She alights from a cab with seventy black and purple anklets clanking about her secular feet, a foreign postage stamp—canceled—perched upon her cheek: a wig of purple and gold caught roguishly up with strands from a cable once used to moor importations from far Cathay; red trousers...an ancient human notebook on which has been written all the follies of a past generation."

As if the spectacle that was Elsa wasn't extravagant enough, a year after arriving in New York she married Baron Leopold Freiherr von Freytag Loringhoven, a German anti-war protestor from Berlin. They installed themselves in the Ritz Hotel, from whence the lady, now Baroness Elsa, made guerilla raids on the culture. The marriage lasted an improbable three years and might have gone on 'til the wheels fell off, except that the Baron committed suicide, presumably over gambling debts.

For Elsa, the splendid period over, it was back to nude modeling and chasing men. The *New York Evening Sun* of January 26, 1916 carried this headline: "His Model and Soul Mate, Too. Artist's Infatuation for Baroness Told by Wife." It seems Mrs. Renee Dixon was suing her husband, artist Douglas Gilbert Dixon, because he had "been almost completely monopolized by his poetic soul mate model, the beautiful Baroness Elsa von Freytag-Loringhoven."

After seeing one of Else's assemblages in Marcel Duchamp's studio, William Carlos Williams went to the infamous jail known as the Tombs, where Elsa was being held for stealing an umbrella, and bailed her out. They began an affair that quickly became too intense for Williams, who was a compulsive womanizer (but only on forays into New York, when he could get away from his home and wife in Paterson, New Jersey). When the Baroness went looking for him in Paterson, Williams had her arrested. Later, when he convinced her to leave him alone, the Baroness said, "Too bad. I could free your mind for serious art."

The stories about her are seemingly endless. At a reception for a then-famous opera singer named Marguerite d'Alvarez, the prima donna announced, "My art is only for humanity. I sing only for humanity." From the middle of the crowd, the Baroness hollered, "I wouldn't lift my leg for humanity."

Once, the Baroness attended a party at the French embassy. In her journal, she described her outfit and allowed as how she fancied the Consul. Besides stamps for beauty marks on her emerald-painted cheeks and eyelashes made of gilded porcupine quills, she wore a "large wide, sugarcoated birthday cake upon [her] head with fifty flaming candles." Elsa mentions that she felt "*just so* spunky . . ." One might say that rather than her cap, she set her "cake" for the Consul. In any event, she had "several ropes of dried figs dangling round [her] neck to give him a suck once and again…"

In 1923, tired of the pretentious New York art scene, and perhaps weary of seeing her sanity debated in the pages of literary magazines, she returned to Germany. But she hadn't counted on post-war inflation and the chaos of a failed revolution. The Baroness was reduced to selling newspapers on the street. In 1926, Djuna Barnes and some other friends took up a collection to enable her to come to Paris. She seemed to be recovering her spirits and getting down to some important work, particularly on her autobiography which she was writing as a series of letters to Barnes. On the morning of December 14, 1927, one of her young lovers sneaked into her apartment and turned on the gas, evidently as a joke. The Baroness never woke up.

As Djuna Barnes wrote, she died because of "a stupid joke that had not even the decency of maliciousness."

Her contemporaries talked and wrote manifestos about art that was an attack on conventional sensibilities. They heralded a new breed of artist who recognized no boundaries between art and life. The Baroness Elsa von Freytag-Loringhoven was the only person who lived up to the ideal, and she did so without trying to—she couldn't have been bothered.

The last thing she wrote attested to the belief that deep within her was "glittering wealth." Perhaps, but the way she lived her life was all richness, "glittering" like "fifty flaming candles." Sixty-nine years after her death, in the 1996 exhibition of Dada art at the Whitney Museum in New York, her art work received its first official praise, being called "a great revelation." §

# Slim Gaillard
# (1916–1991)

Slim Gaillard told a lot of stories about himself and he told them well. As is the case with many such people, especially ones who've been around, he had more than his share of doubters and detractors.

A person with nothing else to do might come up with a mathematical formula to prove that the better the raconteur and more varied the life from which the material is drawn, the more doubt cast upon the stories.

So just imagine Slim in his satin-smooth voice, saying, "Jack Kerouac? Yeah. In San Francisco, him and me got all the women 'cause we were the best looking cats around. Long ago, Jack wrote about me."

And there's *On the Road* to prove it: "One night we suddenly went mad together again; we went to see Slim Gaillard in a little Frisco nightclub . . . crowds of young semi-intellectuals sat at his feet . . . he does and says anything that comes into his head . . . now Dean approached him, he approached his God; he thought Slim Gaillard was God."

Or Slim telling somebody, "Marlene Dietrich? Yeah, she dug what I did." And there's a recording of *The Bob Hope Show*. Bob: "Say, Marlene. Do you know this Slim Gaillard?"

Marlene, unrehearsed, saying simply, "Vout."

Say what?

Slim claimed to have been the first person to speak the word "groovy." Lexicographers might dispute that point, but not that he invented the language of Vout. There was a lot of what was known as

IMAGE: SLIM (RIGHT) AND SLAM PERFORMING "FLAT FOOT FLOOGIE."
© DUNCAN SCHIEDT. USED WITH PERMISSION.

"jive talk," starting in the '30s and lasting until the lyric- and language-challenged rock-and-roll era, and people like Harry "the Hipster" Gibson, Babs Gonzales, and Leo Watson performed linguistic acrobatics, but none flew so high on that trapeze as Slim Gaillard. He wasn't just inventive, he was surrealistically way out there.

How'd this hip, scalawag-ish wit get that way? It would be too easy to ascribe his love of the word and all its possible permutations to a checkered background. All that his background did was provide raw material. Bulee "Slim" Gaillard was born that way, with the predilection for language. Where that birth took place is open to question. Most biographical dictionaries of jazz claim Detroit as the place. Slim said Santa Clara, Cuba. It is true that he traveled on ships with his father, who was a steward. Slim told stories about how, when he was twelve years old, he got left behind in Crete.

Before he started in vaudeville as a tap dancing guitar player, Slim was a boxer and a mortician's assistant. He claimed to have worked in speakeasies owned by Al Capone, who was always nice to him, as he was to other musicians.

In the early '30s, he went to the famous Brill Building to audition for agents in search of "professional amateurs." You had to sound bad enough to convince audiences you were an amateur while simultaneously being good enough to hold their interest. All the people hired made a circuit of vaudeville theatres and radio shows, like *Major Bowes Amateur Hour*.

Gaillard remembered: "I would be a tap dancer one week, play the guitar the next, boogie woogie piano the week after that." Slim's biggest number, recorded in 1938 with bassist Slam Stewart, was "Flat Foot Floogie." Nowadays, this tune, both cool and madcap, is known only to old jazzbos, explorers of obscure musical realms, and fans of Jack Kerouac who happened to see documentary footage of the writer on *The William Buckley Show*: the host, with his usual supercilious air, asks his guest who, for all intents and purposes appears to be asleep, a ridiculous question about the origins of the hippy movement. Kerouac opens his eyes, looks at Buckley, and sings a reply: "Flat Foot Floogie with the floy floy!"

"Flat Foot Floogie," Galliard recalled, "came from a riff I used to play on *Major Bowes*. Then Benny Goodman played it and soon everybody was singing it." Gaillard and Stewart, known as Slim and Slam, had other surrealistic jazz hits, like "Vol Vist du Gaily Star," "Chicken Rhythm," and the original "Tutti Frutti."

After the Second World War, during which he served in the famous segregated black squadron of the Air Corps, Gaillard got with another bassist, Bam Brown, and there came more hits, particularly "Cement Mixer (Putty, Putty)." Slim and Bam were booked for a two-week gig at Billy Berg's Club in Hollywood, and stayed for a year. "Vout," also known as "Vout Oreenie," became so popular, even Ronald Reagan, according to Slim, was talking it.

One night, or early morning, Slim went to an Armenian restaurant and became intrigued by the menu, the writing on which he could not understand. He copied the words into his notebook, went home and put them to music. The result was "Yep Rock Heresy" which was so downright unusual squares figured it had to be "degenerate," and probably "communist-inspired" as well. Thus, the song was banned from several radio stations, and Slim had another big hit. In 1945, he recorded a song called "Genius" on which he sings, plays trumpet, trombone, tenor saxophone, piano, organ, bass, and drums, and tap dances in rhythm. The next year he composed a twelve-minute "Opera in Vout" that was recorded live.

In the late '40s in North America, a mad rush to the suburbs was on; jazz got cool, bop hard, and Slim worked but sporadically. In the early '50s, he was showing off solid musicianship in gigs at Birdland with Billy Taylor and Art Blakey. He made some recordings with Norman Granz but by the late '50s he was back to scuffling. He quit the road after a tour where he had to open for Stan Kenton, which calls to mind Art Pepper's comment in his autobiography *Straight Time*: "I took a gig with Kenton until something came up in jazz."

Gaillard used to frequent a Hollywood restaurant in the mouse hours, to talk with other musicians and dig the comedians telling jokes that they couldn't use in their acts. He was approached by an acting agent, who got him to read for a part. With music gigs scarce, Slim became an actor, appearing in John Cassavetes' *Too Late Blues*. Later, he was in the television series *Roots*.

He continued to play an occasional music gig until the early '60s when the British Invasion and the subsequent Age of Aquarius put him out of work. Gaillard managed a motel in San Diego and eventually bought an apple orchard in Tacoma, Washington. For twenty years, the only time Slim appeared on a recording was with his son-in-law Marvin Gaye. Two of those hands clapping on cuts of "Sexual Healing" are Slim's.

In the early '80s, Dizzy Gillespie visited Slim in his apple orchard, and began a campaign to get him back into music. Dizzy convinced the promoter George Wein to engage Slim, and the result was a summer on the European festival circuit. Then came a steady gig in the Patio Bar of Le Méridien Hotel in Paris. In 1983, he went to London for a two-week date and to record an album with Buddy Tate and Jay McShann, and wound up staying.

It was the return of Slim Gaillard. "I got that old music feeling again," he was quoted as saying. Slim played all over Europe, appeared with rappers on their recordings, had a bit in a terrible movie called *Absolute Beginners* and was the subject of a four-part BBC documentary series. He died of cancer in 1991.

So what made him so hip? It isn't just that he seemed to be able to do everything. It was the way he did it. He was assured and smooth but never, ever arrogant. The very idea of anyone else trying to do that record, *Genius*, would be offensive. Often considered, so unjustly, to be a comedy act, Gaillard was a terrific musician and great singer. For every so-called novelty number there was a serious soulful one, like "Mean Mama Blues" or "Boot-Ta-La-Za."

One of my favourite Slim cuts is "Slim's Jam" featuring Dizzy Gillespie and Charlie Parker. Not only is there a devastating solo by Parker but also a display of Slim's ad libbing in Vout. At one point, Dizzy says he has to go to make another gig, to which Slim replies, "Oh, I was just going to order up some avocado seed soup."

This cut also offers a rare incidence of Bird talking to a peer. Slim saying, "Why there's Charlie Yardbird." There's a whole lesson in cool to be derived just from the way Slim phrases that sentence, the way he stresses the "Yard . . . bird." Bird replies, "Hey, Slim. What's happening, Jim?"

And by the way, a pure glimpse of hip is Parker's solo, which copies but extends that of tenor saxophonist Jack MacVie, a hell of a solo itself from which Parker squeezes that one remaining drop, of what? Soul. It is sexual, is what it is. And in case one has not picked up on that, there's Slim, exclaiming, "Unnhh!"

Maybe that's the thing with Slim Gaillard; an ever-present, behind-the-beat sexuality underlined everything he did. Whether he was singing, dancing, playing instruments, being funny, or inventing new language, he conveyed, without insinuating, the sexual content of things. §

# Tillson Lever Harrison
## AKA Dixie (1881–1947)

It was Constantinople in the spring of 1922, and Tillson Lever Harrison, a small-town Ontario boy nicknamed Dixie, was slated to appear before a firing squad for various transgressions. He had washed up, broke, in Turkey several months before, but was able, being a physician and surgeon, to secure a position at a hospital. Evidently no one wondered why such a competent and knowledgeable individual appeared so scruffy and down at the heels. He had just spent several months in Eritrea, tending to the medical needs of villagers and soldiers opposed to the Italian invasion. Anyway, it is pure Dixie, so to speak, that the hospital to which he was attached was devoted to the care of diseased prostitutes. Harrison wasn't long on the job before he was permitted to resign due to certain "improprieties" (i.e., sexual relations with patients).

Dixie was soon living with the mistress of the head of the Turkish Flying Corps. Deciding to put some distance between them and the boyfriend, Harrison and the woman took flight and attempted to pass over into the lines of Mustafa Kemal Atatürk. While holed up in a mountain village, the pair were arrested and Harrison thrown into jail. The day before his date with the firing squad the British government stepped in to save his life.

But that is only part of the story, one that most people, even most irrepressible adventurers, could dine out on for the rest of their

98 | SCALAWAGS

IMAGE: TILLSON LEVER HARRISON, PHILLIPINES, DATE UNKNOWN.
USED WITH PERMISSION OF THE ANNANDALE NATIONAL HISTORIC SITE.

lives. As for Harrison, there'd been other firing squads. Once in Mexico, during the revolution, he'd literally had his back up against the wall after eschewing the blindfold when Pancho Villa's forces bombed the encampment, providing him the opportunity to flee his Carrancista captors.

Back in Turkey, Dixie again took up with his girlfriend while the British government endeavoured to have him deported. His Majesty had determined that Harrison already had a wife in Malta. Once the notice came through and his passage was booked and paid for by the Crown, Harrison nevertheless borrowed money from several men, telling each that he needed money to pay his way back to Canada. He went on a spending spree at local stores, on credit. He was well set up when he arrived in Montreal for the next stage of his adventurous career.

Just about all of Tillson Lever Harrison is summed up in that anecdote: rogue, adventurer, con man, womanizer, and, a part easier to overlook, hero; he had after all devoted months of self sacrifice as a medical missionary in Ethiopia, a country besieged by an outside force.

A year earlier, in 1921, Harrison had been written up in a Colorado newspaper because he'd performed an appendectomy on a worker in a mine shaft, using a coal-fired lamp, razor blades, and matches. The reporter located Harrison's closest remaining relative, a nephew, back in Tillsonburg. The nephew shrugged off his uncle's exploits, saying, "My father always maintained Dixie was the greatest womanizer, and greatest liar, he'd ever met."

Despite the fact that we live in an age where the farthest reaches of the globe and the strangest behaviour of its inhabitants is available at the press of a button, our age is correspondingly smaller. It's a homogenous time and our adventures are increasingly vicarious. So a person like Tillson Lever Harrison is unfathomable to most of us.

If one were to write a book or make a movie about the Canadian who was the greatest rogue in our history, it would have to be about Harrison. Likewise, were one to write a book or make a movie about Canada's greatest hero, it would be about Harrison—yes, yes, I sense your protests on this point but just you wait (Bethune? He ain't in it.).

So why then has there never been a book, never been a movie? I used to ponder this question while investigating Harrison's life, and lately I've come to realize it is because, like the man's nephew inadvertently explained, the story beggars belief. Tillson Lever Harrison crossed the line.

But the thing is it's all true.

One thing Harrison always did lie about, however, was the date of his birth. He set it back to join armies when he was a kid and set it forward to join military medical teams when he was older. He was in fact born in Tillsonburg, a town founded by his grandfather, in 1881. In 1892, his mother was granted a divorce, a very uncommon thing in those days and a cause for scandal. She cited cruelty, drunkenness, and bigamy. The boy's first act of rebellion was in climbing a tree that was forbidden to him. He tied a yellow ribbon on the top branch. In 1895, he ran away from school and joined the 22nd Oxford Rifles. When it was discovered that he was only fourteen, Dixie was sent home. Not to be denied the dream of adventure, he ran away again and enlisted in the U.S. Army Corps of Engineers and served all 114 days of the Spanish-American War. He was with the army at the battle of Manila where he contracted Asiatic cholera, was left to die in a field hospital, and was even asked where he wished his remains to be sent. It was this experience of neglect that inspired Harrison to become a doctor.

In 1900, his regiment was sent to China where it helped to put down the Boxer Rebellion. There is a year missing—the first of many—in the account of Harrison's story, but by 1902 he is enrolled at the University of Toronto. He was married in 1905 and graduated as an M.D. in 1907. By then the Nevada Gold Rush was on and Harrison became part of it. The next few years are impossible to fit into any chronology—actually, most of the man's life defies strict chronology—but it is known that his daughter was born in Spokane, Washington, that he was a doctor and medicine man with Indians in Utah and that he was, for a time, mayor of Drewsey, Oregon. It is also known that in 1909, he walked out the door of the house where he lived with his wife and child and never returned.

In 1912, Harrison was in China serving as a battlefield doctor with the forces of Sun Yat-sen that were opposing the Manchu Dynasty. In 1913, he was in Mexico, attached to the forces of General Carranza. He became a Lieutenant-Colonel, and was a bodyguard and chauffeur to the governor of Sonora, as well as a surgeon. Later that year he was with the American army again, this time serving under General Hugh Scott at the Battle of Aqua-Prieta in Arizona and in the Utah Indian Uprising; next, it was the Yanqui Indian battle in Mexico, after which Harrison joined Carranza again, but soon aligned himself with Pancho Villa when Villa rebelled. This was the time of the firing squad.

In Mexico, during the later part of 1914, Harrison met veteran soldier of fortune Sam Dreben, the ace machine gunner from Brooklyn who had by then already lost an arm and an eye. "I've seen them all, all the great ones, Terence O'Rourke, Lee Christmas [famous soldiers of fortune], but this kid," Dreben was supposed to have said about Dixie, "makes those fellas look like shoe clerks."

In March, 1916, Harrison was with Villa when the rebel leader fled south after invading the United States and attacking the town of Columbus, New Mexico. It is likely that Harrison had been part of the raid. The men were pursued by General John Pershing.

In 1917, at Calgary, he enlisted in the Canadian Army Medical Corps and rose to the rank of Captain, seeing duty throughout France. He is next rumoured to have served with the French Foreign Legion. It is known for certain that he was on a French medical team battling trachoma and leprosy. Over the next couple of years he left traces throughout the Middle East, in Sudan, and Morocco.

On August 7, 1922 he wrote from Dublin to the Registrar at the University of Toronto seeking written proof that he graduated with a degree in medicine: "A few days ago I arrived here from Morocco where I had a rather unpleasant experience, having been a prisoner among the Moors and sold as a slave. I suffered many hardships, escaped, walked 563 miles along the seacoast to Oran, Algiers…Then worked my way from Algiers to Dublin. For authenticity of this statement you can refer anyone to the "Despache Algerine" of Alger city, 1$^{st}$ week in May, or . . . ."

It was after his Dublin service with the Irish Free State Hospital that Harrison arrived in Turkey. After his return to Canada late in 1922, his experiences are like a collage with pieces missing. He did for a time live with natives in Alberta but in 1927 he was in Vera Cruz, Mexico, on the medical staff of a hospital. From 1929 to 1934, Harrison was in Ecuador, Venezuela, and Colombia.

In 1935 in Trinidad he was employed as head of the medical staff at the Saint Madeline Sugar Company. After several months, he departed the company and the colony "without any notice, and leaving behind a considerable amount of indebtedness both to the Company and Local Trades people . . . ." So wrote the director of the sugar company.

Harrison's 1936 stay in the Cayman Islands lasted only two months, long enough for him to become famous for curing several cases of tuberculosis. He left behind his personal belongings and more bills.

Harrison was back in his beloved China in 1937, with the Chinese National Red Cross. His whereabouts are unknown in 1939 and 1940, but from 1941 until the beginning of 1946, he served as Medical Officer on British Merchant Navy Ships of the South East Asia Command. In March 1946, he took seven years off his age and joined UNRRA, The United Nations Rehabilitation and Relief Agency in Shanghai. He was sixty-six years old. In 1946, he made three trips to escort several thousand tons of medical and relief supplies to areas under the control of the revolutionary forces. Koumintang authorities did whatever they could to try and hinder Harrison's work. At one point, Harrison managed to steal an American officer's uniform that frightened his KMT adversaries and allowed him to continue his journey. After his first trip into the Communist-controlled areas, Harrison was told by the deputy commissioner of the border region, Bo Yibo, that he was a *huo caishen,* a living god of wealth to the people.

In December 1946, Harrison departed on his last trip from Shanghai. He traveled by train, truck, and ox cart, and was attacked, arrested, and beaten. Much of his supplies were stolen. It was necessary for Harrison to break through the ice of ditches to have water to drink, but this was water polluted by manure. He went days without eating. Israel Epstein of the Chinese Friendship Society, a friend of Morris 'Two-Gun' Cohen, the Canadian one-time jailbird who had become the bodyguard to Chiang Kai-shek, saw Harrison during his last days. "His feet were frostbitten—his shoes and blanket had been stolen as part of the harassment to which he was subjected in Koumintang Territory."

Nevertheless, he managed to deliver 280 cases of medical and surgical supplies to the International Peace Hospital at Handan. It is thanks to him that the hospital got its first beds, operating tables, microscopes, and X-ray machines. Even its first electric fan.

Harrison died in his sleep there in Hebei Province at the end of his third mission, on January 10, 1947. As Epstein wrote, "His courage was greater than his worn-out body could stand."

Harrison had been employed as a doctor and surgeon. It was not his job to escort medical and relief supplies but he did so time and again, delivering thousands of tons of materiel.

The Chinese immediately erected monuments to him. International Peace Hospitals at Handan and at Zhangzhou in Henan were renamed in his honour. A month after his death, a memorial service for Harrison was held at the New Asia Hotel in Shanghai. Guest speakers included Soong Ching-ling, who was Chairperson of the China Welfare Fund and the wife of Sun Yat-sen.

His family in Canada was notified of his death but no mention was made of it in newspapers in this country. The Chinese stated that Harrison had died a hero's death, not a liar's, a rogue's, or a con man's.

In January, 1988, the month and year the Chinese mistakenly took to be the 100$^{th}$ anniversary of Harrison's birth, his remains were moved to a new tomb at the Kaifeng Martyrs' Cemetery; underneath a bust of Harrison is an inscription by former Chinese leader Deng Xiaoping. During the ceremonies, State Councilor Huang Hua, who had known Harrison in 1946, said that the entire nation "cherished the memory of his unselfish contributions to the Chinese people."

What, then, to make of this man? He was a scoundrel without peer and a selfless hero, a selfish wanderer and a one-man Medecins Sans Frontières, a loner who gave his life for a nation. How did he balance his own contradictions? What did he think about facing those firing squads, deserting one woman after another, looting the coffers of Caribbean companies? What was on his mind when he made those arduous journeys through blizzards across war zones in his adopted land? What did he think about during all those nights on ships and buses and planes, going from one adventure to the next?

Of course, it would be easy to draw conclusions, say, for instance, that he risked his life at the end to atone for decades of mischief. But that would be spurious nonsense, because Harrison was always risking his life to save people, on a score of battlefields. He even doctored lepers when no one else would go near them.

We'll never know what he thought.

Unless . . .

Dixie was known to keep a journal from an early age. People report seeing him writing in a journal. A few scatted newspaper reports quote from his journal. He is rumoured to have stashed these things all over the world. Maybe someday, one or more journals will surface. Perhaps that seems unlikely but, then again, that's the way it should be, for anything concerning Tillson Lever Harrison is unlikely. §

# Sadakichi Hartmann (1867–1944)

The image of the romantic literary rogue persists even in this conventional age, when the average writer is thoroughly housebroken and relentlessly respectable.

Your serious 21$^{st}$ century scrivener, while deep-down clinging to the vestiges of the notion, simultaneously takes refuge in the reality of hard, lonely work. Even Lord Byron spent most of his time in a room, all alone, scribbling, they will sniff. He wasn't always swimming the Hellespont or seducing seventeen-year-old countesses.

To mention the average contemporary scribe in the same sentence as Lord Byron is surreal, but to toss the name of Sadakichi Hartmann into the mix smacks of magic realism. Hartmann would have taught Byron to dance on his clubfoot, offered some suggestions on how to improve *Childe Harold's Pilgrimage,* and run away with the countess, not to mention the silverware.

As for today's writers, Sadakichi wouldn't recognize the breed. He did, after all, hobnob with Walt Whitman, Stephane Mallarme, Paul Verlaine, Gertrude Stein, Ezra Pound, Amy Lowell, Edna St. Vincent Millay, and just about everyone else in the arts from the 1880s to the 1940s. He even met Jack Kerouac in a bar near the Columbia University campus in 1941 and read the first stories of the unpublished nineteen-year-old author.

His raucous ways, refusal to compromise, his vagabondage, the

SADAKICHI AS THE COURT MAGICIAN IN THE 1924 FILM *THE THIEF OF BAGDAD*. DIRECTED BY RAOUL WALSH, STORY BY DOUGLAS FAIRBANKS. COURTESY OF THE LIBRARY OF CONGRESS.

dozens of children he sired—thirteen in legal wedlock alone—his stints in jail, his thievery and knavery, his reputation as the King of Bohemia in the early twentieth century, and all the other things he did on the side, have obscured his accomplishments as an important writer, daring playwright, flamboyant poet, and prescient art critic.

Hartmann was the first writer to take photography seriously as an art form. In 1900, he published the first comprehensive history of American art, a work that remained the standard text well into the 1950s. He touted photographers Edward Weston and Alfred Stieglitz long before they became famous, promoted the then-unknown painters George Bellows and Thomas Hart Benton, and was an indefatigable lecturer and critic. As well, Hartmann was an accomplished dancer, a master of judo, and a pretty good painter and photographer himself. Ezra Pound declared, "If one hadn't been oneself, it would have been worthwhile being Sadakichi. Except my constitution wouldn't have withstood the strain."

"Sadakichi is singular," Gertrude Stein maintained, "never plural."

He was born in 1867 on the island of Desima in Nagasaki harbour. His Japanese mother died in childbirth, and the boy was taken to Hamburg by his German father. There he was raised by a grandmother and an uncle, attended several finishing schools and was expelled from each of them. Placed in a naval academy, he rebelled, and was shipped off to America.

He lived in New York and Philadelphia doing odd jobs and studying in libraries. In 1883, he was befriended by Walt Whitman, and translated the good grey poet's German correspondence. At the beginning of their relationship, Whitman seemed to love Sadakichi like a son. But Hartmann presumably misquoted the poet and raised money for a bogus Whitman society. Shortly before dying in 1891, Whitman was heard to refer to Hartmann as "that damned Japanese"—the only recorded incident of Whitman uttering a curse.

During the late 1880s, Hartmann traveled many times to Europe and apprenticed himself to theatre and dance companies. It was at the Hof Theatre in Munich that he spied on Mad King Ludwig. Hartmann would sneak into the Royal Box in the dark, hide under a seat and take notes, which he later turned into newspaper articles.

In Paris, he was frequently at the home of Paul Verlaine, often when Verlaine wasn't there. He became intimate with the great poet's long-suffering wife. They would linger in bed indulging in post-coital gossip about Verlaine's affair with Arthur Rimbaud. Hartman had noticed that Verlaine chewed his pencils. After the poet died, Hartmann and the widow would sit up in bed chewing pencils that they later sold as mementos of the famous old poet who loved the famous long poet.

Once Hartmann stole a fan from Anatole France and tried to sell it back to him. France wrote him a nasty letter that Hartmann bartered to a collector for dinner for two at Maxim's, his companion a demi mondaine, also provided by the collector.

Hartmann's rap sheet included arrests for stealing taxicabs, seditious behaviour, numerous charges of disturbing the peace, anarchism, vagrancy, obscenity (busted in Boston for his play *Jesus Christ)*, and fifteen or twenty other charges. He was also an admitted peeping tom, although with all his women—those he chased and those who chased him—voyeurism seems inconsequential.

He was thrown out of the mansion of Henry Clay Frick for telling the industrialist, "You are a great man in a small way." It has been suggested that it was Hartmann who convinced Alexander Berkman to choose Frick when he was looking for an assassination target. On another occasion, he was thrown out of a concert by a protégé of Franz Liszt, for hollering at the pianist, "Is all that necessary?" To ushers hustling him up the aisle, Hartmann said, "I am a man needed, but not wanted."

In 1923, Hartmann met Douglas Fairbanks, who told him, "You have the eyes of a saint; the rest of your face is like that of a villain." Fairbanks cast him as the court magician in *The Thief of Bagdad*.

"Hartmann didn't need make-up," quipped critic Kenneth Rexroth. The much-underrated poet Benjamin De Casseres referred to Hartmann as "a grotesque etched in flesh by the drunken Goya of Heaven."

In the early '40s, Hartmann was taken up by a Hollywood circle that included John Barrymore, W. C. Fields, artist John Decker, and screenwriter Gene Fowler. The first time Fowler met Hartmann, he thought he "looked like a forgotten potato and had the astringent wit of an unfrocked prior of the Neo-Gothic Age." Hartmann had come to pay a call on Fowler in his office at the RKO Studios. Hartmann took one look around the back lot and spoke his first words to Fowler: "Hollywood is the back porch of a dream." John Barrymore urged Fowler to write a book about Hartmann, telling him, "Here is your chance to chronicle a living freak presumably sired by Mephistopheles out of Madame Butterfly."

It is doubtful that this circle appreciated what Hartmann had been and had done. There is no indication that they read any of his pioneering works on American art or his interpretation of Japanese art for a Western audience, no sense that they knew his poetry or his plays. One tends to want to chide them for that, and for regarding Hartmann as little more than a funny-looking reprobate with a scandalous past ("See that tall, skinny old man? He once danced with Isadora Duncan.") On the other hand, the reputation of a scandalous past is not such a bad thing, and when the past is that scandalous, that variegated, it would be difficult to expunge.

In 1944, Hartmann, carrying the blood of both of America's then-enemies in his veins, grew weary of being harassed by federal agents on the west coast, and rode a Greyhound bus to St. Petersburg, Florida, where one of his daughters lived. There, in the spring of that year, he died, seated in a living room chair, reading poetry. §

# Al Jennings
# (1863–1961)

We're in the Big Yard at the Ohio State Penitentiary in 1897. The new fish, Alfonso Jackson Jennings, is walking the perimeter, old cons assessing him; he's already a legend. Al Jennings is one of the old breed, a gunslinger, a rustler, and a rogue. It's common knowledge he once outshot Frank and Jesse James. He's in for robbing trains; did it the old-fashioned way, with a gang on horseback. It's not his first jolt, either. It's claimed the man is a lawyer, too. The joke is he's a lawyer *gone bad*.

Jennings sees another guy looking at him hard, but the man doesn't look like a rounder. He's kind of nondescript. Maybe he's what's called a gay-cat. Maybe he's looking for a daddy in this rough place. But there's something familiar about him.

"I believe," the man says, "we met down in Panama, a few years ago." He introduces himself as William Sydney Porter. The two had indeed hung out in Panama when both were on the lam—Porter from a charge of embezzling from the bank where he worked in Austin, Texas; Jennings fleeing a murder rap, having gunned down a man in Kansas.

They recall sitting on the porch of a Panama City rooming house, telling stories; Jennings did most of the telling. "I was standing around in Dodge City one time with Bat Masterson and some of the boys. An actor wearing a stovepipe hat got off the train. Bat pulled his gun,

ALFONSO JACKSON JENNINGS, 1924. COURTESY OF THE LIBRARY OF CONGRESS.

said, 'I'll plug that hat.' He fired and the actor fell down dead. 'Guess I shot too low,' said Bat."

While in the joint, Porter encouraged Jennings to spin more yarns. Porter wanted to be a writer and Jennings was his first serious reader. Jennings told Porter about growing up in Virginia, crossing the country of Oklahoma Territory with his parents, and eventually taking up the life of a rustler, horse thief, and bandit. There weren't many other lines to pursue except that of lawman, and that was considered to be even more dishonest.

While in prison ten years earlier, Jennings had begun reading and taking correspondence courses. He continued his studies upon release, and eventually became the first lawyer in the Territory, but he resumed his life of crime after his brother was killed. It was during this period that he met Porter in Central America.

After Porter was done fictionalizing Jennings' stories, the latter would arrange with guards to have them smuggled out and mailed to magazines. The stories were all rejected. Jennings advised Porter that the endings were the problem: "Make the endings a surprise."

Jennings told how a couple of his friends had snatched a little kid and held him for ransom. Porter had written the story straight and sent it out. It came back rejected just before the embezzler was released from the penitentiary. Jennings urged him to rewrite the thing and make it funny. Make the kid so obnoxious that the bad guys want to get rid of him, but the parents don't want him back. Porter said he'd redo it that way.

And he did. Porter went to New York City and changed his name to O. Henry. He made the story funny and it was published as "The Ransom of Red Chief."

Jennings was released in 1905 and knocked around the world, using various aliases. In 1907, he was granted a pardon by President Theodore Roosevelt and became an evangelist, preaching against crime. It was a good scam and Jennings enjoyed it for a time, but finally gave it up because of the people with whom he had to associate: "Some of the preachers were worse than the outlaws."

Jennings next turned to politics and ran for governor of Oklahoma, claiming that if he was elected, he'd be honest for a year, "Which is a hell of a lot longer than anyone else has been honest."

He lost, and the experience soured him on politics. "A train robber," Jennings maintained, "wouldn't associate with the average politician."

Jennings went to Hollywood and got work as a technical advisor on westerns. Most of his advice wasn't taken. After he'd been in town a few years and developed contacts, Jennings was able to make his own westerns. Some of this silent footage still exists and reveals his films to have been unlike anything being made. They were exactly as it must have been in the "wild" west. The scenes are stark, the good guys decidedly unheroic, the bad guys even less so. When a shoot-out occurs, Jennings portrays the act with all the accompanying confusion. He made thirty silent films, but none was successful. In Jennings's words, the public wanted "to see a clean-cut fellow with a tablecloth around his neck."

He gave them anti-westerns. It took nearly eighty years before another filmmaker came even close to showing the west as Jennings had done. If you want to get an idea of what Jennings accomplished, watch Jim Jarmusch's *Dead Man*, especially the scene near the beginning when Johnny Depp gets off the train at Machine, Wyoming and takes his walk up a main stem filled with mud and horse shit, pariah dogs, and hookers who don't resemble Miss Kitty from *Gunsmoke*.

Time passed and Jennings continued to hustle. He got busted a few times for working the short con and even made an attempt at the straight life—chicken farming in Tarzana, California. Meanwhile, he wrote up some of his exploits and others wrote up some of his exploits and his fame spread around the world. Or so Jennings claimed, although few seemed to believe him.

It is fascinating how some people who have lived outrageous lives beyond the mainstream are invariably deemed liars. This has been going on forever, and it happened with Jennings. One of his severest critics was western historian Stuart Lake. Yet Lake was the man who believed everything told him by that pathological liar and Republican party hack, Wyatt Earp. It's Lake who was responsible for turning a cheap, white-trash crook into Wyatt, the "brave, courageous and bold."

So Lake wrote that Jennings was deluded if he thought he was a legend. Then, in 1936, the French writer Blaise Cendrars (who himself has been called a Baron Münchhausen) arrived in Hollywood to oversee the filming of one of his books. At a farewell party in his honour, Cendrars met a young writer named Sanora Babb, who happened to mention being from Oklahoma. Hearing this, Cendrars became excited and asked if she knew Al Jennings, the famous outlaw. "Me, I know *everything* about him," said Cendrars. "He is a legend."

Babb knew the old bandit, and this chance encounter at a party led to Cendrars meeting Jennings in Hollywood at four in the morning. Jennings made Cendrars a present of one of his six-shooters from the old days. When Cendrars got back to Paris, he translated Jennings's book *Through the Shadows with O. Henry.*

In the 1940s, Jennings sued the producers of *The Lone Ranger* radio show for $100,000 because of the way he was portrayed. Jennings told the judge that he was particularly exercised because "The Lone Ranger caught me like a common criminal. He shot the gun out of my hand! And me an expert!"

In the '50s, he was portrayed by Dan Duryea, in silver spurs, in the film *Al Jennings of Oklahoma.*

In 1962, shortly before his death, Jennings was interviewed by Stanton Delaplane of *The San Francisco Chronicle*. "I'm a killer," he told the reporter. "I remember one fellow, he kept saying 'Don't shoot me, Al. Don't shoot me." After that I always shot them in the throat so they couldn't talk back." Photographs accompanying Delaplane's article show the ninety-eight-year-old "killer" looking like an animated, one-eyed version of the aged Dustin Hoffman character in *Little Big Man.*

The last thing Al Jennings shot was a television set that was showing *Bonanza*. §

# Alfred "Lash" LaRue (1917–1996)

IMAGE: "LASH" WITH HIS FAMOUS BULLWHIP.

It was the winter of 1966, and I was in a Cuban restaurant on Washington Avenue in Miami Beach, eating a *medianoche* in the late afternoon. By the third cup of coffee, I was down to reading the three-line crime items in the back pages of the *Herald,* and there it was: "Former Western Movie Star Busted for Vagrancy." The vagged cowboy turned out to be none other than my very first hero, the man with the bullwhip, the original man in black, Lash LaRue.

As a kid in the 1950s, I had seen his B movies recycled from the '40s, met his sidekick Al "Fuzzy" St. John, and read *Lash LaRue* comic books. I can still recall the cover of one of them: Lash, in the centre of some dusty western boomtown street in his black garb, with black hat cocked to one side, black scarf, silver-studded gun belt, two mother-of-pearl-handled revolvers, and a rolled bullwhip in his right hand. As for the movies, even at age seven or eight I realized they were awful at best but redeemed by Lash's presence. What an antidote he was to the others, all those white hats of the '50s western craze: Hoppy, Gene, and Roy. Somehow I knew life wasn't like that, that all the guys with the white hats weren't all that good; they weren't going to really turn away from ranchers' daughters and kiss horses. Those fellows looked like Methodist preachers, Lash like the Dead End Kid who absconded with the collection plate and headed west. He often started out as the bad guy, as in *The Cheyenne Kid,* and ended up the good guy, despite himself.

Sure those were romantic childhood notions. Then I went to the jail to meet him and quickly discovered that my ideas were immature—only because they were too restricted to contain the hustler, grafter, con man, womanizer, scandalous gossip, and unrelenting scalawag that was Lash LaRue.

As an adult, I might sum him up this way: the French, not having guys like Lash LaRue, had to invent pale facsimiles or mythologize petty criminals. And then there is Camus' *L'Etranger* walking the beach in Algiers smoking his cigarette and laying down a mental blueprint for existentialism. Lash would have laughed at his notions, taken the cigarette out of his mouth with a crack of the bullwhip, and stolen the dork's girlfriend.

I went to the jail over in Miami and announced my business. The sergeant looked over his sheet and said, "Don't know anything about any cowboy named Lash but we picked up a drunk carnie called Alfred LaRue."

Into the dayroom, the cop led a guy on the short side of medium with thick eyebrows who needed a shave and was dressed in baggy khakis and a Hawaiian shirt. Lash looked around warily. The cop pointed to me and Lash came over, sizing me up along the way; he seemed to be considering the angles and his escape route.

I told him I didn't want anything but that I dug him as a kid and just happened to be in town, etc. He seemed to warm to the part about watching his movies. I said something about there probably having been a lot of people coming by from television and the papers but he shook his head, said there hadn't been a soul. When I mentioned having worked in the carnival myself, he told me to sit down and take a load off.

I bought the coffee and he started talking. It wasn't normal conversation, it was a torrent of words (from him) that didn't stick to the main channel but leaped the banks and knocked down saplings and the neighbour's fence and made for the highway. Me, I was just there to direct the flow when I thought it was safe. But his brook didn't babble. His speech might best be described as jive talk with biblical, scatological, and criminal content.

Lash had spent a lifetime on the hustle, and had probably devoted more years to the carnival than to motion pictures. "You know, I started out in gangster pictures? I was always cast as the bad guy."

"Gee," I said. "I wonder why?" Lash was the kind of guy who, when he paid for something in a store, the clerk at the register always held the bill up to the light.

He'd done so well in those early films that he was sent to audition for the second lead in *Red River*. "I could have had it too but there were certain acts I would not perform. And that's why Montgomery Clift got to be a big star and not me."

Then he began talking about Maureen O'Hara in salacious detail and was reminded of one of his wives, who was a trick rider, "in more ways than one, son." Other wives were brought to mind and Lash referred to them absent-mindedly like they were car keys he had misplaced. At one point, he asked me about my mother. "She must be 'round about my age, right?" When I told him it was probably true, he wanted to know if I had a picture of her. Coincidentally, I had just been to General Delivery at the post office and found a letter from my mother with a photo enclosed of her and my cousin, at his wedding. I showed it to Lash, who said, "Hmm, nice-looking woman, if you'll pardon my mentioning it. She get along with your father?"

During all this talk, he would quote the Bible, and a particular passage might remind him of a pinhead or a half-and-half from one ten-in-one or another.

After the cowboy movie craze and a short-lived television series that consisted of spliced-together sequences from his old movies, Lash started working state and county fairs with a whip act. A significant amount of his time was spent avoiding women with whom he had been involved. As the years passed, he was performing the act in carnival sideshows and was eventually reduced to working at the lowliest of carnival jobs, setting up and tearing down tents, and operating rides. During these years, the late '50s and early '60s, the bottle had proven a steadier companion than any woman.

He was arrested while stumbling down a street, hollering, "Kill me, kill me. Put me out of my misery!"

He talked, and I mostly listened, for three hours, and Lash would have kept at it and I would have gladly been his audience for three more, except a beautiful (if gaudy) woman, a cooch dancer from the carnival, showed up to pay his bail. I walked out of the jail and down the street with them. There was a neon sign outlining a martini glass. Lash invited me to go into the bar with them for a drink or two but I declined, knowing he was only being polite.

I never saw him again but was happy to learn that Lash moderated his drinking and got back on the hustle. He even made more movies and earned some money on a circuit of festivals devoted to western movie cowboys. His comeback film was called *Hard On the Trail*. Lash signed on innocently enough and got a week's work riding around in black, jumping on and off horses, cracking his whip, and bursting through cabin and hotel room doors. But unbeknownst to Lash, this turned out to be a porno flick. There was another "Lash" involved for the sex stuff.

He appeared in a remake of *Stagecoach* with Johnny Cash, who admitted he had gotten the "man in black" idea from his early hero, Lash LaRue.

My mother, whose picture Lash had admired, died on May 21st,

1996. While I was talking with my father a couple days later, he said, "Your old pal, Lash LaRue, died the same day as your mother." I looked up his obituary. The reporter called a woman who was thought to be Lash LaRue's wife. "Oh, we were married, all right," she said. "But he had ten other wives, maybe more." §

# Ignacz Trebitsch AKA Trebitsch Lincoln AKA Chao Kung (1879–1943)

He was called an "international vaudeville act"—too dangerous for Hitler to know.

When he died in 1943, his name was Chao Kung. He had been born in 1879 as Ignacz Trebitsch. Between those dates, he used more than a hundred aliases, chief among them Trebitsch Lincoln. In 1920, he was sketched thusly by a *Daily Telegraph* correspondent: "There is something almost Olympian about this man's scoundrelism . . . I have heard it variously suggested that he was in the movement as a Bolshevik, as a British and as a French spy. Possibly he was all these . . . the world will watch with interest to see at what point this really remarkable rogue will crop up next."

Where he cropped up next—a week after that article appeared—was in a Berlin jail on a conspiracy charge, Lincoln having been one of the chief instigators of the Five Day Revolution in Germany. He was next seen plotting the worldwide right-wing uprising known as the White International, but that's getting ahead of the story.

Ignacz Trebitsch came from a prosperous Jewish family south of Budapest who gave him an orthodox education and a genetic predilection to madness. Trebitsch had a compulsion to seize attention

GENERAL PHOTOGRAPHIC AGENCY / HULTON ARCHIVE / GETTY IMAGES.

and a pathological need to travel. His first public attention came by way of Budapest police records, in which he was enrolled as a thief. Soon afterwards, he was wanted in Trieste as well. He later claimed to have gone to South America to get out from under these charges.

In London he was taken in by a missionary society, the purpose of which was to lead Jews to Christianity. Lincoln eventually converted, attended a Presbyterian seminary, and became, in Montreal, a street-corner preacher—preaching in German, Hungarian, Yiddish, and English. Later, he was ordained an Anglican deacon and took over a parish in England, but quit, changed his name to Lincoln, and, in 1910, was elected to the House of Commons as a Liberal MP for Darlington. To keep this latter achievement in perspective, it should be noted that Lincoln—besides being a petty crook and, what was worse in the England of that time, a Jew—had never voted in a British election and wasn't even a naturalized citizen when he secured the nomination.

Lincoln didn't run for election again, because multifarious transactions of a questionable nature were catching up with him. He initiated more of the same, mainly involving Romanian and Galician oil wells. He dragged his wife and family around Europe, frequently abandoning them in Bucharest and Budapest, as he would later do in New York and Sarawak.

When World War One began, Lincoln offered himself as a double agent to British Intelligence. He was turned down. So he made the same proposal to the Germans, who gave him some minor assignments. Later, he fled to New York and wrote newspaper articles in which he claimed to be a great international spy. Lincoln was arrested and held for extradition, but he escaped. After being at large for a month, he was captured, shipped back to England, and convicted of fraud. He served three years in Parkhurst Prison on the Isle of Wight.

After his release, Lincoln penetrated right-wing journalism circles in Germany and fell in with Colonel Max Bauer, who had been a member of the General Staff during the war. After the Five Day Revolution—a bloodless coup—Lincoln was made head of propaganda.

The best indication of Lincoln's reputation at the time is revealed in an anecdote concerning the poet and journalist Dietrich Eckart and Adolf Hitler. Hearing of the coup, Eckart and Hitler hired a plane and flew from Munich to Berlin. In the Hotel Adlon, Eckart caught sight of Trebitsch, whom Hitler did not know. Eckart grabbed his friend's arm and led him from the hotel, saying, "That's one guy you don't want to know." Hitler told the story for the rest of his life—how Eckart had shielded him from bad influences.

After the collapse of the Revolution, Lincoln fled Berlin with false papers supplied by the chief of police. After more arrests, escapes, and involvement with the White International in Hungary, Lincoln surfaced in China, made his way to Ichang and connected with warlord General Yang Sen. It is believed that Lincoln engineered the General's takeover of Chungking.

The next several years in Lincoln's life seem to exceed the bounds of any possible linear description, being more analogous to an exploding kaleidoscope than anything else. He was in almost constant motion—leading a Chinese delegation through Europe, advising three more Chinese warlords, fleeing arrest one more time with an Austrian passport issued under the name Leonard Tandler. Somehow he managed an interlude in Monte Carlo, posing as a gambler with a surefire system for baccarat. Naturally, he went broke. But that never stopped Lincoln—or Tandler, or Vilmos, or Ludwig, or Keelan . . .

Lincoln landed next in the Dutch West Indies, where he abandoned his wife and children again because there was something that required his attention in Armenia. And on it goes.

His career at this time was described, by a journalist catching him on the fly, as "an international vaudeville act." But viewing it from a distance, Lincoln seems less a grinning song-and-dance man than a grim-faced tragedian; a top that spins like that has to go out of control. Such desperate people, if they're aren't murdered, usually choose suicide or religion: Lincoln chose religion. At the Astor House in Tientsin, he "made the great renunciation. I quitted the world. I forced the doors of the lunatic asylum open—and walked out."

He left the mad house and walked right into the arms of Madame Blavatsky. But the Theosophical Society couldn't hold him. The fickle Trebitsch embraced Buddha and took up residence at a monastery in Ceylon. Evidently Lincoln's renunciation didn't cure him of the disease of peripatetica, and he spent another rambling decade that included begging, importuning, and being arrested. He managed to get ordained as a monk at a monastery near Nanking in May, 1931 and took the name Chao Kung. From this date until his death, he never again appeared in public in western garb.

Chao Kung spent two months at a cabin in an orchard with a Buddhist friend in Naramata, British Columbia. He was subsequently arrested in England, Germany, and Austria. He collected a dozen converts who followed him back to Shanghai, where he established the Buddha House on Great Western Road.

Back in Shanghai, he was shadowed by intelligence agents from at least three governments, who kept bumping into each other. He had mysterious dealings with a known Bolshevik agent. When the Japanese seized Shanghai, Chao Kung offered his services. At the beginning of World War II, he was approached by the Nazis. He proposed going to visit Hitler, where he would cause the three wise men to materialize through the walls of the Fuhrer's office whereupon they would show him the way to victory and world peace. The Nazis declined the gift of the magi.

Chao Kung spent his last years in Shanghai, living in a YMCA room with three steamer trunks filled with what he claimed to be important secret documents. He walked around the city dodging bombs, and people pointed him out as a nut with a past.

He died of "intestinal problems," a man who had lived a gaudy, tatterdemalion life that in the end signified nothing.

No sooner was Chao Kung's body carted away to a potter's field than several mysterious armed men appeared at his tiny YMCA room to go through the "important secret documents." They left with each of the steamer trunks. §

# Eliza Lynch (1835–1886)

Eliza Lynch was born in County Cork in 1835. Everything she ever said about her childhood, or at least whatever was recorded, was a fabrication. It is true, however, that her family was lucky enough to get out of Ireland during the potato famine, and to flee to Paris. Supposedly she met Victor Hugo when she was thirteen and the great man told Eliza she was a genius. Chopin wept when Eliza told him she had no intention of following a career as a concert pianist.

But she was beautiful, a fact no one during her entire life ever disputed. In 1850, at age fifteen, Eliza married a French Army officer and followed him to Algiers. She was bored, and fancied by most of the men in the garrison. Unfortunately, one of them was her husband's commanding officer, and one morning, after the two men adjourned to the dueling grounds, Eliza ran off with a young Russian cavalry officer. Naturally, he was rich and handsome, and he had a mansion in Paris to which they fled.

It was the Second Empire, and for a while the couple led a glittering, fabulous life. But only a few months after they'd settled in, the Crimean War broke out and the officer had to return to Russia.

And what was a gorgeous seventeen-year-old girl with an hourglass figure, flaming red hair and a mansion to maintain to do? She became one of *Les Grandes Horizontales*.

Her introduction to the world of courtesans was provided by Princess Mathilde, cousin of Napoleon III. Soon Eliza had dozens of rich and titled gentlemen after her. Eliza had gaming tables installed

A YOUNG ELIZA LYNCH. USED WITH PERMISSION OF SOUTH AMERICAN PICTURES.

on the first floor of her mansion so that her admirers could lose their money while waiting their turn to climb the stairs.

Meanwhile, in Paraguay during these years, Francisco Lopez, son of dictator Carlos, was coming of age. As a boy, Francisco's favourite reading matter was a book about the suppression of the revolution of Túpac Amaru II, last descendant of the Inca Emperor. Francisco especially liked the part about Túpac watching the execution of his wife and children before he was himself mutilated and beheaded.

As a young man Francisco, according to the American Ambassador Charles Washburn, was a "licensed ravisher." Washburn also provides a description of the future dictator. "He had a gross animal look. His forehead was narrow, his head small with the rear organs largely developed. The few teeth in his mouth were black."

In 1853, Francisco led a delegation to Europe—they were the first Paraguayans to travel abroad. When he was presented to Empress Eugenie, she turned her head and vomited on an ormolu desk. He was introduced to Eliza by a friend who had sampled her favours and bragged about it. Eliza had observed the fat young man giving orders and throwing his money around.

Francisco was smitten the moment he laid eyes on her, but after she was finished with him upstairs, he was helpless. For her part, Eliza realized this was the main chance. She would have looked forward to a comfortable life as the mistress of one Minister after another, but now she saw fabulous riches, an entire country for the taking.

She became Francisco's mistress. The delegation started back to Paraguay upon receiving news that Francisco's father was ill. In Asuncion, she was greeted with outright hostility, despised by the women, shunned by Francisco's family.

Francisco had probably painted a grandiose picture of his hometown, a lively metropolis set in a tropical paradise. In reality, Asuncion was a hole with shacks and open sewers and no public works. Most of the people had nothing, a few had everything. Eliza vowed to clean the place up and redistribute the wealth. She certainly took from the rich—and gave to herself.

Eliza encouraged Francisco to have municipal buildings constructed. He'd order projects but never see them through to completion. When their son was born, the event was announced with a one-hundred-and-one-gun salute, and eleven buildings collapsed in downtown Asuncion. Francisco did oversee the completion of two structures: a mansion for himself and a mansion for Eliza. The road he caused to be built between them was the first straight road in Paraguay.

Eliza encouraged Francisco to take mistresses and have affairs. This kept him diverted and out of her bed. She even served as his procuress. Eliza had her own lovers, chosen from the diplomatic corps.

Eliza was able to exercise almost complete control over Carlos, who assumed titular control of Paraguay when his father died. Cunningham Graham, who lived in Asuncion, wrote: "Obstinate as he was, he was entirely dominated by his clever, beautiful and unscrupulous mistress."

The most devastating war in the history of the Americas began when Eliza and her paramour Vasquez Sagastume, the Uruguayan ambassador, had the idea of seizing a Brazilian steamer loaded with gold. When the Brazilians complained, Eliza urged Francisco to attack them which, of course, he did. It was Eliza's scheme to make him Emperor of South America.

The two countries went to war. Then, Francisco attacked Argentina, and Uruguay entered the war on the side of Argentina. Eliza organized fancy balls. Women guests were forced to wear their jewellery, and forced to donate their jewellery, ostensibly, for the war effort. The best pieces, Eliza sent out of the country in the diplomatic pouches of her lovers, to be deposited in her banks in Paris or London.

The fighting, sometimes known as The War of the Triple Alliance, lasted five years. Three armies were unable to beat one, because the Allies were even more incompetent than Paraguay. Francisco had no idea of warfare and was interested primarily in torturing prisoners. Later, when there were not enough prisoners to torture, he began inventing conspiracies and arrested people he tortured into making false confessions. Most Paraguayan military victories occurred when Eliza diverted her attention from gathering jewellery to take command.

She began "buying" up land. She made offers that landowners could not, if they wanted to live, refuse. She also seized the holdings of the thousands who were arrested. By the time she was twenty-five years old she owned more real estate than any other woman in the world: in addition to dozens of town and city properties, ten million hectares of countryside.

The country was devastated by the war, by disease, hunger and Eliza's rapaciousness. She encouraged the cult of the Virgin in the little town of Carupe. It seems that fifty years earlier, a woman had prayed to the Virgin and when her prayer was answered, placed a gold bracelet at the foot of the Virgin's statue. Others began to do likewise, and to leave jewellery in hopes that their prayers would be answered. Before fleeing Paraguay at the end of the disastrous war, Eliza gathered up half a century's worth of jewellery, "for the war effort."

But she was brave. In the last days, she directed military operations at headquarters while her husband cowered in a specially built bunker. Eventually, Francisco deserted in the night, and the next day, Eliza took sixty men and went looking for him. While he was in hiding, she moved the capital to the town of Piribebuy and began affairs with anyone who might be able to assist her after the inevitable collapse.

The Brazilians took over on August 15, 1869, and established a provisional government. Francisco was still on the run. He was killed in March 1870. Not long after, Eliza was captured in the jungle; she was wearing a ball gown.

A million people had died in the war. To keep the people from her, Eliza had to be imprisoned on a Brazilian gunboat. She was allowed to flee South America, and headed for London, where some of her money was cached. Next she went to Paris, and eventually returned to Buenos Aires, where she saw a play based on her life.

Five years after the end of the war, in hopes of retrieving some of her property, Eliza dared a return to Paraguay. She received a heroine's welcome from the people; the government deported her.

The next several years of her life are a blur. It is known that she went to the Holy Land and that she made yet another trip to Buenos Aires. From 1876 to 1886, when she died at age fifty-one, nothing is known of her life. Some said she went back to her former profession.

She was buried in Père Lachaise in Paris.

But death did not put an end to the adventures of Eliza Lynch. Her reputation and that of her husband began to be rehabilitated in 1936, when Rafael Franco assumed power and made Paraguay South America's first fascist state. He needed another dictator to serve as an historical precedent, and who better to choose than Francisco Lopez?

A cult developed around Eliza Lynch, and was encouraged by Alfredo Stroessner, who took power in 1954. He built a monument to Eliza but was lacking her remains. This situation was rectified in 1961 due to the efforts of an underworld entrepeneur, a Lebanese-born Paraguayan named Teofilo Chammas. He paid off guards at Père Lachaise Cemetery, stole her body and returned it to Paraguay. Her remains now rest in a mausoleum dedicated to her. More fitting to her memory, perhaps, is the statue of Eliza Lynch out near the airport at Asuncion. She holds aloft a tattered flag of Paraguay; at her feet, appropriately, is a dead Paraguayan. §

# Adah Isaacs Menken (1835–1868)

"She did not rouge but played some deviltry with her glorious eyes." —Charles Reade

She came into Virginia City, Nevada, on the Wells Fargo stagecoach in the early 1860s, sitting up top with the luggage and facing backwards because she wanted to keep an eye on her stallion, which was being transported in a following wagon. It was the horse that she rode at the thrilling finale of *Mazeppa*, bareback and in pink tights. The illusion of nakedness that had left the men, and a few of the women, swooning from coast to coast, would soon be the case in Paris and London.

The story got around, and maybe it was true, that the stagecoach had been attacked by Comanches who weren't interested in the strong box or the stallion, but in the star passenger. It was further attested that the young lady went off behind some cottonwood trees to negotiate with her would-be captors. The story may be apocryphal, but with Adah Menken one can never be sure. She was then only twenty-six years old and had already led a dozen lives.

According to the reporter with the Virginia City *Territorial Enterprise*, a fellow who called himself Mark Twain, Menken had the effect of "a vast spray of gas jets." She was "a magnificent spectacle," not a star but "a whole constellation."

A dozen lives.

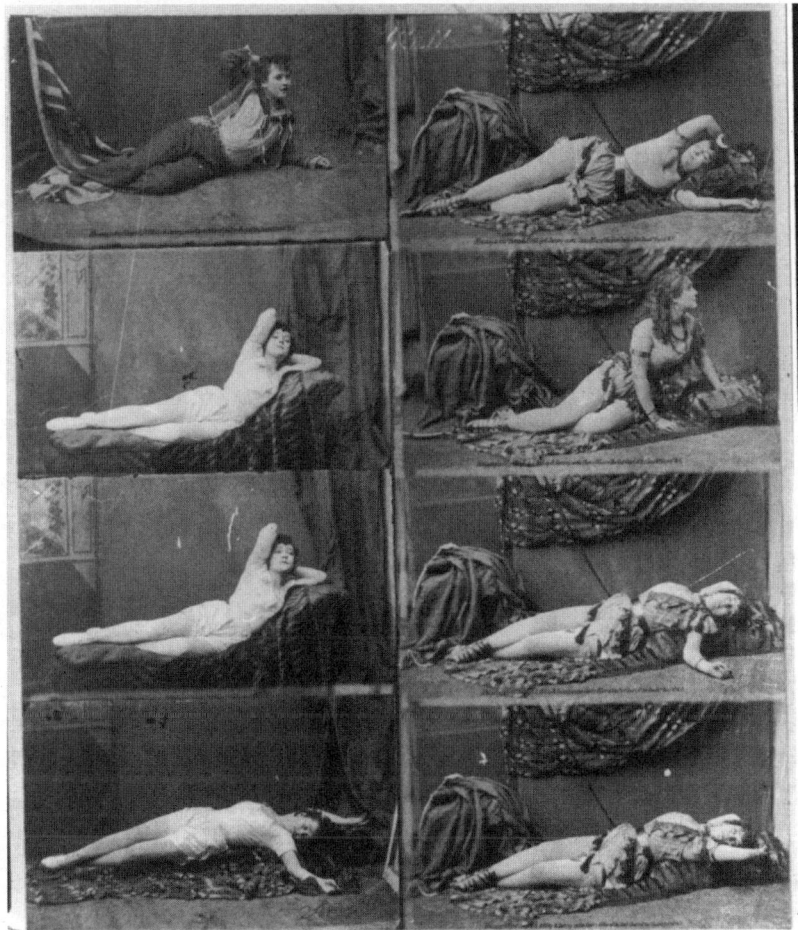

ADAH MENKEN, 1866. COURTESY OF THE LIBRARY OF CONGRESS.

No one knows for sure what her real name was or where she was born. The two leading theories are that her father was named either McCord or Theodore, and that she was born in 1835, either in Mississippi or just outside New Orleans. Biographers who maintain her father was McCord insist that her mother was Creole; those of the Theodore school, that her mother was part Negro. Other, earlier, theories had her born in New York, France, or the Caribbean, of various racial mixes.

She was attached, at age eight, to the ballet school at the French Opera House in New Orleans, and proved to be a natural. When she was fifteen, the age she later claimed to have been when raped by her mother's boyfriend, Adah went to Havana as a dancer. There she was hailed as The Queen of the Plaza, and conducted an affair with Juan Clemente Zenea, a nobleman and popular poet. The affair ended when Clemente displayed outrageous jealousy, and Adah departed for Mexico. On his deathbed in 1871, the poet admitted that Adah Menken had been the love of his life.

After a successful tour of Mexico, Adah returned to America, became a striptease artist, and took up poetry and the study of languages. At the age of nineteen, supposedly in Galveston, Texas, she married a musician named Alexander Isaacs Menken, and converted to Judaism. Her husband was mortified that she smoked cigarettes in public. He wanted her to settle down and raise a family, but Adah was having none of it. She left Menken, but hadn't got around to divorcing him when she married John C. Heenan, the bare-knuckle heavyweight champion of the world. "I just thought men were supposed to take care of the details," she told the press during the scandal that ensued. "I mean, like, divorce."

Fortunately for Adah, the press was unaware that she was a bigamist twice over. She did get married in Galveston but not to Menken. Him she married in Livingston, Texas. The Galveston betrothal occurred two years earlier. Facts about her first husband, other than that his name was W.H. Kneass, are lost to history.

Adah and John C. Heenan fought physically when not dueling poetically. A century before Muhammad Ali, Heenan was dissing his opponents in verse. Menken was insulted when it was suggested that she helped him out.

After divorcing Heenan, she married Robert Newell, literary editor of the *New York Sunday Mirror*. Menken must have reckoned that she needed a more proper sort of husband. Newell was a rigid, conventional writer, and a Puritan. He installed Adah in his home in Jersey City and forbade her to leave; that was a woman's place, after all. Adah managed a week of it before exiting from a second-storey window and making for Manhattan.

Her last husband was a gambler and confederate agent named James Barkley. Adah left Barkley after three days because he wanted her to cancel an upcoming engagement in Paris.

What man could have held her? She was a free thinker and libertine, an actress, painter, sculptor, and, probably, the world's first glamour queen. After getting away from Heenan, she had taken to the boards again, starring in *The Italian Wife*. She had a poetry reading act, recited Shakespeare, and impersonated Edwin Booth declaiming the Bard. Adah also appeared, in blackface, as Mr. Bones in a minstrel show. While starring in Baltimore, she was arrested by Federal agents and held as a confederate spy. She was released a week later, after swearing an oath of allegiance.

About this time Adah began a liaison with Roger Blondin, who had astounded the world when he walked a tightrope across Niagara Falls. She placed a caveat on his proposal of marriage: he had to let her cross the falls with him. He replied that he was afraid her beauty would distract him and they would both plummet to their deaths. They made a tour of music halls before splitting up.

She made her fame in *Mazeppa*, which was based on a Lord Byron poem. At the end of the play, the hero, a brave Tartar, escapes on a wild horse. Until Adah, Mazeppa had always been played by a young man, and a stuffed dummy was used in the escape. Menken, however, insisted on doing it herself, in pink tights. She got a great review in New York from her friend Walt Whitman.

But it was in San Francisco that she caused the biggest sensation. Impresario Tom Maguire promoted her appearance at his opera house by writing, "Miss Menken, stripped by her captors, will ride a fiery steed at furious gallop onto and across the stage and into the distance."

Menken knocked the Civil War off the front page of the newspapers. Yet, bored, Adah left San Francisco at the height of her fame and notoriety. In London she set records at the box office, but the press was unkind and condescending. Punch called her "a puff of a Jewess."

Eventually, she took *Mazeppa* to Paris where she was again a sensation. Adah also appeared at the Théâtre de la Gaîté in *Les Pirates de la Savanne*. Rich men lined up for her favours, and the first she chose, with a nod toward her idol, Lola Montez, was King Charles of Württemberg. Rumours spread of a morganatic marriage, but before she could get around to ruling the tiny kingdom, Adah met and fell in love with Alexandre Dumas, père—the King of Romance.

He was the Lion of Literature, a big-bellied big spender, down on his luck and growing old, but after taking one look at Adah backstage, he told himself that D'Artagnan would ride again. Some people insisted that Dumas was past it, but as a series of notorious photographs intimates, the affair was more than platonic. The pictures of them together were not meant to be circulated, but not only did they reach the general public, some unscrupulous photographer used look-alikes to produce obscene versions of the originals. It is likely that Adah was chased out of Paris through the machinations of Alexandre Dumas, fils.

Next, it was to London, where Adah was lionized by Charles Dickens, Charles Reade, Dante Gabriel Rossetti, and Charles Swinburne, who told her, "A woman with such beautiful legs shouldn't bother about poetry." Menken was the only woman who was ever capable of rousing Charles Swinburne "to scratch," as she put it; the only woman to whom he ever made love. And could not desist, evidently. His poem about her, "Dolores," is infamous. Charles Dickens wrote an introduction to a volume of her poetry.

But Adah missed Paris and returned to France. She was to appear in a show but was in ill health. When two months on the beach at Le Havre failed to restore her, Adah took to bed in a small hotel in Paris and never left it in life. She maintained the lie of her conversion to Judaism to the very end, August 10, 1868, when a rabbi made Kaddish over her. Her religion forbade a post-mortem. The cause of death was given as "a complication of diseases."

"Too much living" might have been a more apt diagnosis. She

was thirty-three years old, and looked a tired fifty-three. In a photograph of Adah, at eighteen years of age, she looks almost too beautiful.

The death certificate was issued under the name Menken Adele Isaac Barclay. Her legend has never died. In our time, we have seen reference to her in the Broadway musical, *Gypsy*; Ruth Roman and Roxanne Berard portrayed her on *Bonanza* and *Gunsmoke* on television, and Sophia Loren was Adah Menken in the movie *Heller in Pink Tights*. Playing somewhere in the world tonight is a stage show about her.

Despite her travels and romances, her triumphs and affairs, her studies and excesses, the stories of her appeal, the legend of Adah Menken was best expressed by a western historian who, in the late 1800s, wrote that there were still men around in the West who recalled the wild old days, who bragged of having a drink with Kit Carson or looking Jim Bridger in the eye. But the man who could one-up them all was the one who could say, "Yes, well, I saw Adah Menken in pink tights ride that horse across the stage." §

# Count Geoffrey Potocki de Montalk (1903–1997)

I was sitting in the lounge of a hotel in Christchurch, New Zealand. On the commons beyond the window were leafy trees and an Anglican Church, all very peaceful. What a place to have been home, if only briefly, to a character like Count Potocki de Montalk.

"What band is he with?" asked the waitress, pulling me out of my thoughts and setting my drink down.

"Band?"

I glanced at the book. There on the cover, looking at me and the waitress with a dark-eyed stare, was the Count. He had perfectly symmetrical features, dark thick eyebrows, a straight nose, and a chin one would have to call manly. He looked strong but at the same time strangely vulnerable. The Count wore a cape clasped at the neck over a flowing white shirt, his dark hair hung in waves to the middle of his chest.

"You think he's cute, eh?" I asked the waitress.

"Oh he's more than cute, I assure you."

"How would you describe his appeal?"

She made a sound way back in her throat.

"I'm sorry to say that he died back in 1997."

"Live fast, die young and leave a good-looking corpse kind of thing, yes."

I didn't have the heart to tell her that the Count, no Goth Rocker

ILLUSTRATION BY DEREK VON ESSEN. USED WITH PERMISSION.

but irascible scalawag, inveterate enemy-maker and pretender to the throne of Poland, although he might have been beautiful at one time—okay, he was beautiful at one time and had lived fast—died old, very old, and very much alone.

I'd been hearing stories about the Count since the first time I went to New Zealand back in 1990. Before that, I'd come across him in memoirs of London in the 1930s but never as a poet or a printer, always as a character whom one crossed the street to avoid if only one managed to spot him in time. Later I ran into people who'd known him. Once, I might have seen him in the small town of Hamilton on the North Island. Was he that old man in a cape hobbling around a corner? I like to think it was. After all, how many ninety-some-year-old men in New Zealand small towns of the time wore capes? And the Count had lived in a bed-sit in Hamilton. But, no, maybe the cape was a raincoat and it was another old man, one who didn't speak ten languages and hadn't been in prison for writing dirty poems and was not a king.

"The course of my life is an indictment of the whole dishonest racket which calls itself democracy." The Count believed that and lived it.

That life began for Geoffrey Wladislas Vaile Potocki de Montalk in Auckland, New Zealand in 1903. He had a happy first few years before his mother died and her place was taken by the wicked stepmother. He was a boy attuned to beauty, coming of age in one of the world's most beautiful places. But it wasn't the beauty of nature that stirred his soul.

After high school, he was taken on by a law firm but fired when overheard in a pub discussing a will he had prepared. He next studied theology, and his father, upon hearing the news, wrote to tell him, "God help the church."

But Geoffrey quit his studies to work as a teacher. It was necessary to travel by horseback between schools, and the future Potocki was fired because he couldn't stay on the horse. He was married at twenty-four and had a daughter who was expected to die because she weighed less than four pounds at birth. Geoffrey wouldn't allow the infant to be kept at the hospital. Instead he took her home and wrapped her in flannel soaked in olive oil. She survived, but two years later he abandoned her and his wife to go to London to be a poet. He didn't see his daughter again for fifty-six years, by which time he'd had several other daughters by several other women. And he had a new name.

In London, Potocki indeed wrote poetry and played the role of poet, a creature that he cut from whole cloth, a pretentious, overbearing, argumentative scribbler of archaic verse. In England in the mid-1920s, Potocki was a bad 1820s poet. As for his claims to royalty, well, he was a Potocki, one of the first families of Poland, and a descendant of mystic adventurer Jan Potocki. Not long after leaving

New Zealand he was befriended by an actual Polish nobleman, traveled with him to a Polish enclave in Lithuania and was thrilled when peasants greeted them with low bows and cries of "Good day, Mighty Lords." He wanted more of that.

In 1932, he gathered translations he'd done of Paul Verlaine's "Idylle High Life" and Rabelais' "Song of the Codpiece" and together with some poems he'd written about an amorous adventure concerning his fellow New Zealand poet, Alex Fairburn, decided to publish them in a pamphlet. The Count intended to print the poems himself but handed over the manuscript to be typeset. The printer immediately contacted Scotland Yard and Potocki was arrested and charged with publishing obscenity.

He was sentenced to six months in prison during what was called, in *Books in the Dock,* "the most extraordinary obscenity trial of the century."

It was also a travesty. The judge turned out to be a poet himself and even worse than Potocki. As well, he was a bit of a sexual hypocrite, as was later revealed. Potocki appeared in capes and sandals, and the courtroom was filled with young women. The newspapers called him "strikingly handsome."

The judge overlooked the fact that both translated poems were widely available in France in the originals and that Potocki's manuscript had been "published" only in the strictest and most old-fashioned sense of the word. It hadn't been printed; it hadn't even been typeset. Nevertheless, the judge advised the jury of their "duty to fight smut."

When Potocki was released he was the same, only more so. His dress became even more flamboyant and he now claimed to be heir to the throne of Poland and Hungary. He continued to write poetry, most of which he published himself, and to print pamphlets wherein he attacked democracy, communism, Jews, and most of his fellow poets. No one knows where his anti-Semitism originated.

Potocki added to his list of enemies in 1936, the beginning of the Spanish Civil War, when he began publishing an occasional literary and political journal, *The Stet.* In 1939, when the police came to arrest him for a violation of the blackout law, he barricaded himself in his flat. When they finally managed to enter, Potocki fought with them and was charged with assault. Upon appearing before the judge, Potocki gave his occupation as King of Poland. He got two months.

In 1943, Potocki was summoned to court again on another matter but refused to appear, citing his busy schedule as King. The Special Branch once arrested him for disturbing the peace by distributing a pamphlet about a massacre of Polish intellectuals and officers by Russians at a place called Katyn. His pamphlet was generally regarded as just another fantasy. It was not until 1990, and the release of previously sealed material in the Russian Archives, that the Katyn Massacre was shown to have been real.

Potocki began to wander Europe, calling on one girlfriend after another. No matter where he was, alone or with people, every morning he said his prayers to Apollo, in Sanskrit.

In the 1950s he settled in Draguignan in the South of France, where he continued his pamphleteering and conducted his arguments with the world. Potocki also continued writing his poetry and a striking thing can be noted in this later verse. In the midst of doggerel would appear a line that might have come from that lofty realm where he claimed his muse had permanent residence. For instance, the last line of the following:

> A universe of lazy-moving dreams
> Green bubbles for cities, bright
> Fishes stars unborn
> Wind billowed grass—before God
> Thought of flowers.

In the 1980s, Potocki returned to New Zealand for the first time in nearly sixty years. He moved around between friends and relatives. This became his pattern, traveling from France to New Zealand and back. New Zealand provided an entirely new field in which to make enemies and to ensure his legendary status. He had gangs of admirers. "We called him 'The Chief,'" one of them remembers.

Potocki made a big show of being King of Poland and Hungary but admitted, now and again, a flaw in his claim: the fact that he was not Catholic.

He professed to despise the modern world and everything about it. "He hated America, particularly," Donald Kerr, a rare-book librarian and world traveler, told me. "And anything that came out of it." One day, Kerr remembers, The Count wanted to phone a daughter, "Countess Something or other." Not having a phone, Kerr directed him to a neighbour. When Potocki hadn't returned after a couple of hours, Kerr went looking for him.

"It was raining. I panicked, thinking the King of Poland and Hungary is feet and arms up in a drain in Laingholm…"

After scouring the area, Kerr went to see his neighbours: "Where's Potocki? Where's the Chief?"

And there he was, "sitting on a green La-Z-Boy, eating pizza and watching a film on television about John F. Kennedy. I immediately thought: 'Now there sits a survivor.'"

The Count survived until 1997, when he died in a nursing home in France. He had traveled back to France alone three years earlier, at age ninety-one, eager to do battle. He got his press ready in Draguignan. The world was going to hell in a handcart, and he, King of Poland and Hungary, survivor from another age and time, was still ready to take on anyone and anything. He knew he was right, and to hell with everyone else. §

# Elizabeth Gilbert AKA Lola Montez (1821–1861)

"I have known all the world has to offer," declared the woman known as Lola Montez, just before she died. "*All!*" She was a shameless scoundrel and a liar who would have made Baron Münchhausen blush, but she was stone honest when she made that deathbed claim.

She was the deadliest of *femmes fatales,* the vamp of all vamps, and made no distinction between counts and comic opera con men, world famous composers and back country hostelers. She even toppled a king.

The woman who would be known to the world as Lola Montez was born Elizabeth Rosanna Gilbert in Ireland in 1821. Early on, she was remarkable for both her looks and her mendacity. "An honest thing never passes from her lips," said a clergyman in England.

According to the sister of Lord Auckland, Governor General of Bengal, she was, at fourteen while living in India, "a great beauty...that drives other women with pretensions in that line quite distracted."

Men were distracted, too, and she caused such a ruckus in boarding school that her mother had to return to India to retrieve her. On board the ship taking her to India, Lola's mother began a romance with Thomas James, an officer of the East India Company. Upon

IMAGE: COURTESY OF THE LIBRARY OF CONGRESS.

landing, James took one look at her daughter, who was half his age, and that was it for Mrs. Gilbert.

James and Eliza Gilbert eloped and were married a couple of months later. James got sent to India again and was posted far from town, which enabled his young wife to carry on with other men. James sent her back to England. On the way, she humiliated him with a noisy shipboard romance.

James filed suit for divorce. Eliza had two other court cases pending and must have realized that no respectable life was left to her. She could choose between adventure and a nunnery. Thus, it was goodbye Eliza, *hola* Lola.

She went to Spain, stayed four months absorbing the culture and studying dance, and returned reinvented. She seduced the Spanish consul at Southampton, who introduced her to the Earl of Malmesbury, whom she also seduced. How she was able to convince these men and thousands of others that she was Spanish remains a mystery. The Earl told his diary that Lola was "the widow of Don Diego Leon, who had recently been executed for his part in a plot to overthrow the government of Queen Isabella II."

It would be wrong to maintain that all of Lola's sexual conquests were strategic. While it is true that the Earl was her introduction to the London stage, she also picked up men she fancied on the street.

Her opening night at Her Majesty's Theatre caused a riot. Half the audience was in a swoon, the other half was hurling vegetables. She was either a sultry Spanish sensation or an Irish fake, a genius or an embarrassment. She inspired journalistic debates and full houses. But she had to leave London when too many people showed up in the audience who knew her as little Eliza Gilbert or as Mrs. James.

Lola went on a European tour, taking her Spanish dances as far as St. Petersburg. On her way back, stopping at a roadhouse just over the Polish border in Germany, she saw a newspaper story about Franz Liszt. She studied his concert schedule and set her cap. The flamboyant Hungarian genius was the most famous man in Europe. Lola caught up with him in Dessau. She laid her famous blue eyes on Liszt and that was that. No matter he was living with Marie d'Agoult and that they had three children; within an hour of meeting, Lola and Liszt were together in bed. Eventually they took an apartment in Dresden.

The affair lasted three months, or until Lola was thrown out of Dresden for "scandal-making." She started a barroom brawl when she punched a male Italian opera singer in the mouth. Lola was handy with her fists, the knife in her sleeve, and a whip, when she could reach one. Years later, Liszt would write, "All other women pale beside her."

From Dresden she went to Paris and became the mistress of a publisher who was later killed in a duel.

She was thrown out of Prague for assaulting a police officer, out of Berlin for whipping a groper on the street, out of Baden-Baden for sitting with her skirts halfway up her thighs.

In Munich, thwarted in her attempts to get a performer's permit, she used her contacts to get an audience with the then-popular King Ludwig I. As the story goes, when Lola was ushered into the royal presence, the stalwart King, then sixty, had to hold firmly to his desk to steady himself.

His Highness gave Lola the once-over, pausing at her bosom, and asked, "Nature or art?" Lola ripped open her bodice and said, "You be the judge?"

Three days later, Ludwig was confiding to his diary: "I'm like an amorous boy of twenty, I'm in the grip of passion like never before . . . I am happy. My life has new vitality. I'm young again. The world smiles on me."

Yes, but it wouldn't smile for long, poor man.

Whatever Lola wanted, she used her mental and erotic control over Ludwig to get. Realizing his weakness, Lola allowed the King sexual intercourse near the beginning of their tumultuous sixteen-month affair, then teased him until near the end. When she finally relented the second time, it was on condition that he make her a countess. In the meantime, Lola permitted Ludwig to worship at her feet—literally. When the fetishistic urge came upon him and he wasn't able to satisfy it with the actual feet of Lola, he made do with a marble cast he'd commissioned of her right foot resting on a marble pillow.

Lola's control over the unfortunate monarch was so great that besides making her Countess of Landsfeld, he bought her houses, spent a fortune on jewellery, and let her advise him on policy. Eventually he was almost incapacitated with love and Lola Montez was running Bavaria. While the King dithered, she was spirited away by rogue ministers.

Once word reached the people that the adventuress had gone, order began to be restored. But dressed as a boy and escorted by two of her student lovers, Lola made her way to the palace and had a three-hour private meeting with the King, who gratified himself at her feet and gave her money. She vanished into Switzerland and they never saw each other again.

When the people of Bavaria learned that Lola had returned, even briefly, there were new uprisings. They ended only when Ludwig abdicated his throne.

Lola continued to get money from the ex-King for years. She married a few more times, but neglected to divorce. Having fallen on evil times, she returned to the boards, first as a dancer to packed houses. Lola Montez was, after all, the woman who had brought down an empire. She danced all over the world, made fortunes and lost them. She became an actress—a better actress than dancer, by all accounts. She had dozens more affairs and was in and out of court on assault charges.

During a tour of Australia, she took offence at a mean-spirited editorial and challenged its writer to a duel. Unlike other men who had backed down, this one found her in a saloon and attacked her with a whip. Lola had taken to carrying her own, and they lashed away at each other. When their weapons were seized, they fought with fists. The journalist fled.

Lola Montez discovered spiritualism and Christianity and forswore her wanton ways, but she always remained devoted to lying. She took a small flat in New York's Greenwich Village where she suffered a paralyzing stroke. She recovered, only to be felled by pneumonia. She died in January 1861 and is buried in Brooklyn.

Chiseled on her tombstone are the name "Mrs. Gilbert" and the words "aged 42."

It is ironic that this woman, who had used a dozen different names, and been married numerous times, was buried under a name she had never used. A further irony is that Lola, who had always shaved years off her real age, got her comeuppance from the stone mason who carved her tombstone and made her three years older than she was in fact. She was only thirty-nine. But in those thirty-nine years, Lola Montez took all the world had to offer. *All!* §

# Jean–Frédéric Maximilien Comte de Waldeck (1766–1875)

On the occasion of his one-hundredth birthday, Jean-Frédéric Maximilien, Comte de Waldeck, led an American journalist to his fifth-floor painting studio in Montmartre. The young woman was winded by the climb whereas the Count, over six feet tall, ramrod straight and breathing easily, apologized for not being as sprightly as he used to be. "I sleep well and eat like a wolf but my legs are lazy these days, due to an old rattlesnake bite."

That was in the year 1866. Waldeck was perhaps born in Paris, or maybe Vienna, but most likely in Prague. He was four years old when Napoleon was born. He proceeded to show the journalist mementos and tell her stories. There was the picture that Danton had given him before his date with the guillotine. He visited Marie Antoinette in prison. Then there was the time, after escaping from a battle in Africa, he began to walk with five companions across the continent. The Count alone made it to the Cape. But that, he said, was another story.

The old man was full of plans. The French government had recently bought fifty-six drawings from him but insisted on paying an annuity instead of a lump sum. The Count was vexed, and promised the journalist that he would live a long time to spite the government.

The woman wanted to visit him again the next month but the Count put her off, saying he was going to New York in hopes of financing a massive glass diorama he wished to produce that would display the entire history of science. He had approached P.T. Barnum for financing, and when the showman asked how long it would take, the Count said he needed two years. Barnum shook his head, "You'll never live that long."

He did.

How does one approach anything resembling a chronology with a person like this? There have been no books about this curious specimen and, consequently, it is necessary to piece together fragments, as Waldeck had to do with antiquarian artifacts in various parts of the world. One commentator has written, "By the time he was fifty years old, he had traveled the world, been involved in forty-two revolutions and had lived the life of a hundred men."

Forty-two revolutions?

Who knows.

It does seem fairly certain that he had sailed on an ornithological expedition with the explorer-naturalist François Le Vaillant (and years later rescued him from the gallows in France). His main chore on the voyage was drawing birds. In Paris he studied with Jean-Louis David, the premier painter of his day. He fought in Napoleon's African campaign, was on hand for the siege of Toulon in 1793 and accompanied Bonaparte's Army in Egypt. So audacious was Waldeck that he didn't hesitate to use his drawing abilities to forge Napoleon's signature on a cheque. He was found out, however, and brought before The Little Corporal who demanded the Count copy his signature on a folded sheet a paper. After Waldeck had done so, Napoleon unfolded the sheet and showed it to the forger. "Condemned to three months imprisonment in Vincennes," was what Waldeck read. But Napoleon was amused by this scalawag and had him released after two weeks.

Later, Waldeck joined Robert Surcauf's privateering crew in the Indian Ocean.

In 1819, he encountered Lord Cochrane (on whom the novelist Patrick O'Brian based his great character Captain Aubrey) and sailed with him to South America. Cochrane's task was to organize a navy for Chile in its war of Independence with Spain. After a year or so, Waldeck quarreled with Cochrane and deserted, wandering north, eventually reaching Central America and the ruins of Copan, the sight of which caused a change in his life. He became entranced by the temples and tombs, and vowed to return.

In 1820, in Dublin, at age fifty-four, he was married for the second time. The next year his thirty-year-old wife gave birth to a son. Waldeck had several other children scattered across the world. That same year, a bookseller and publisher in London hired him to engrave the plates for the English edition of Antonio Del Rio's book on Palenque. Del Rio's drawings further stimulated Waldeck's interest in the Mayan world. In 1825, he left his wife and child to take a job as a hydraulic engineer in Mexico. This way, Waldeck figured, he'd be in proximity to various ancient sites. The job didn't work out and after incredible hardships and adventures, the Count found himself working as a freelance in Mexico City, living frugally, sending part of his earnings back to his wife and saving the rest for an expedition he planned on making to Palenque. It would not be until 1832 that the sixty-six-year-old Waldeck was able to begin his expedition.

The Count stayed in the town of Palenque for a year, traveling to the site of the ruins along a trail carved out of dense jungle. He spent another year in a hut he built at the base of a monument that to this day is known as the Temple of the Count. There he produced a hundred finished drawings and scores of sketches.

Picture him nearing seventy, sleeping on the ground at one of the rainiest places on earth, plagued by virulent insects day and night and by thieves whenever he should turn his back. He had to spend hours each day hacking away at the flora or the jungle would reclaim his campsite. Cholera broke out in nearby Campeche and in 1834, a revolution started in Tabasco. Waldeck took time away from his explorations to paint portraits to make ends meet; money promised him by various nobles was not forthcoming.

After two years, Waldeck moved to Uxmal and Ocasingo, spending another year examining these ruins. He was seventy years old when he arrived back in Europe. 1838 saw the publication of his book *Voyage pittoresque et archeologique dans Yucatan, 1834-1836*. Waldeck was loudly castigated and labeled a fantasist, albeit by people who had never been to the sites Waldeck visited. What most provoked their ire were reproductions by Waldeck of elephant friezes. As well, they said his drawings were inferior.

The attacks have never really ceased. Although not many people these days have ever heard of the Comte de Waldeck, those who know the name are Mayan "scholars" and their criticisms of the man have to do with his drawings of elephants and his belief that the sites were the work of people from other civilizations who had traveled to southern Mexico and Central America. In the 20th century, those latter beliefs were adopted by researchers who would be called Diffusionists. These people compared figures on Mayan friezes with those on ancient buildings around the world. Waldeck, seeing elephants on the friezes, likened them to Hindu carvings. Not only are they *like* Hindu carvings, they are identical representations. Only scholars with Mayan specialities deny this, saying they represent "rain gods." Yes, rain gods that coincidentally look just like elephants! Many naturalists believe that there were once elephants in that part of the world.

It's trendy to worship the Maya because, to academics of a certain political orientation, the ruins represent the glorious achievement of a proud indigenous people. In actual fact, the temples were ordered built with slave labour conscripted by a bloodthirsty oligarchy, and the slaves who survived were sacrificed in ceremonies during which their masters took hallucinogenic enemas but that, as the Count would say, is another story.

Waldeck lived a huge life, told fantastic stories, and was bursting with plans until the day he died. Naturally, such a person's very being must have caused many another to feel inferior, even though he was always gracious and charming—maybe because he was gracious and charming. Imagine meeting such a person and listening to his stories. The man had been everywhere and done everything but didn't use his life as a club. If you had met him when he was seventy-eight years old, he might have introduced you to his new wife, age nineteen. They had their second son when the Count was eighty-four. If you felt small, that was your problem.

When in his nineties, Waldeck made the heliogravures for a deluxe edition of erotic drawings from the Renaissance known as *Romano's Positions*. After Waldeck's death more of his erotic drawings were published to accompany an edition of Aretino's sonnets.

He kept on working and scheming. Not long before he died, Waldeck completed a three-volume encyclopedia of American archaeology. In the evenings he attended dinner parties and hung out at cafés in Paris. He died of a heart attack at such a café when he turned to watch a pretty girl walk by. He was one hundred and nine years old.

One writer's remarks about Waldeck's work as an explorer might serve as a summation of his entire life: "He lacked the cautious approach." §

# Bernarr Macfadden (1868–1955)

If Bernarr Macfadden is remembered at all these days, it's as a physical culture crank from the round-iron-dumbbell past, a barefoot old coot who preached the wonders of wheat germ. That's the way he was, too, or partly the way he was. It is not acknowledged that most of the tenets of healthy living that he advocated are taken for granted today. Nor are there many who recall that he revolutionized magazine and newspaper publishing.

If Macfadden's childhood had been a little more comfortable it might warrant the "Dickensian" label. When he wasn't sick in bed, he was toiling in the fields. Born in Missouri in 1868, his parents died when he was still a child and he was shuffled among a series of severe relatives. By comparison, his years in orphanages were almost a vacation. It was a childhood devoid of any kindness or affection. He hit the road when he was twelve, riding freight trains. Somewhere along the line, he discovered physical fitness, and went at it with the fanaticism he would approach everything. The young man was probably the only hobo in North America who carried Indian clubs when he rode the side-door Pullmans.

When he was in a town and working a job, he'd walk to work barefoot, carrying a twenty-pound iron bar in his shirt. He was a water boy and a woodcutter, a construction worker and a miner. In Saint Louis he joined a fitness centre and soon was on his way to

MACFADDEN, AGE 25. COURTESY OF THE LIBRARY OF CONGRESS.

riches. The first prerequisite was to change his names. Born Bernard Mcfadden, he dropped the 'd' from the end of his first name and replaced it with another 'r,' his reasoning being that Bernarr sounded like a lion's roar, and he made the "mc" a "mac" because that sounded more masculine.

He had some success as a wrestler, and started various gymnasiums in the Midwest before hitting New York, where all those flabby subway sitters spelled opportunity. He advertised his health enterprises by holding press conferences where he posed in the nude and ranted against doctors, white bread, prudery, and corsets, and promoted exercise, long walks, fasting, and scanty clothing.

In 1899, Macfadden began what would become a publishing empire by bringing out the magazine *Physical Culture,* a vehicle through which to spread his gospel. He also worked on his five-volume *Encyclopedia of Physical Culture.* As well, Macfadden churned out hundreds of magazine articles and pamphlets. He wrote numerous books on exercise and healthy living, a treatise on eye care, and another on milk that is still in print.

His first magazine made him a well-known and controversial figure in American life. Macfadden was constantly being sued for sending "obscene" pictures through the mail, photos of scantily clad men and women. He organized public exhibitions of beautiful bodies that were often shut down by local prudes. Furthermore, Macfadden preached that sex was not a reason for guilt; that it was, instead, healthy and one of the joys of living. He himself certainly practiced it assiduously without guilt, and could have done millions more dumbbell lifts were his time not taken by wrangling over lawsuits brought by women. When Macfadden's magazine empire expanded in the 1920s, his editors took it upon themselves to keep any young female employees away from his office.

Having noted that his magazine readers sent in confessional letters, he came up with the idea of printing confessions on any topic: health, work, love, sex: anything, as long as it was lively. Thus, *True Story* magazine was born. It was an immediate success, and was followed by *True Detective, True Romances, True Experiences,* as well as *Ghost Stories, Your Home, The Dance, Model Airplane,* and numerous others. There were one hundred and fifty million people in the United States in the late 1920s, and each month forty million of them bought a Macfadden magazine.

Those same years a witty saying made the rounds of New York:

"Don't tell my mother I work on the *Graphic,* she thinks I play piano in a whorehouse." The tabloid scandal sheet was the rowdy brainchild of Bernarr Macfadden. The *Daily News* had the highest circulation in the country, and Macfadden thought he could do even better with a paper of his own. And he did. The *New York Evening Graphic* was the muckraker on the corner, a three-card monte dealer of a newspaper, the guy in the trench coat with girlie photos pinned to the lining. It may have been seedy, but it was more interesting than the rest of them. Just as Macfadden was the first to popularize the use of photographs in magazines, he was the first to ever publish a cartoon in a newspaper. He had a knack of hiring talented people, like Florence Perkins and John Huston. He gave Walter Winchell his first column and when Winchell moved on, the column was taken over by Lou Sobol, who in turn was replaced by Ed Sullivan.

During the Depression, Macfadden started the first of several penny restaurants in New York. There were two levels to these establishments; in the basement, you could buy a basic healthy meal for just a cent; on the first floor a larger healthy meal went for five cents.

Macfadden kept up his physical culture stunts. If there were no important early morning meetings scheduled, he'd walk barefoot from his home, twenty-five miles out of the city, to his office. One day he hiked in toting a forty-pound bag of cement on his back.

After going to England to escape legal hassles, Macfadden returned to America with his second or third wife, Mary Williamson, who had been a champion swimmer. He thought Mary would be the ideal mate to represent him before the public. She became fed up with his attempts to regiment her life; her rebellion took the form of drinking, smoking, and eating pastries. She bore him several children, none of whom grew up to be the beautiful, strong and happy specimen he wished for. After they separated, Mary made suing him her life's work. When his fortunes declined and Macfadden claimed he could not meet his various financial obligations, she insisted that he had buried cash in tin boxes all over the country. Macfadden said the charge was ridiculous.

In December 1947, when Macfadden was eighty years old, he

was having an affair with a woman in her thirties known as Rosebud. They had met in New York at a sermon Macfadden was giving as the minister of a religion he had thought up called Cosmotarianism. Meanwhile, he was keeping company with another woman, forty-two-year-old Johnnie Lee McKinney, who as a girl had read his *Physical Culture* magazine.

On their first date, Johnnie Lee feared Macfadden was going to rape her, but then she told herself that, given his age, that was impossible. Macfadden got her down on the bed, unzipped his trousers and revealed what Johnnie Lee later described as "the most exquisite sex organ I had ever seen on a man."

They were soon married. She told the press that she was attracted by the octogenarian's "sex magnetism."

Macfadden insisted they live apart in order to keep the romance alive. Before too long, his wife realized this meant that her husband could keep his *other* romances alive. One day, she walked into his apartment unannounced, to find him in bed having sex with Rosebud.

The two fought and reconciled for several years before finally separating. In the meantime, Johnnie Lee accompanied her husband while he pursued his various projects. He ran for governor of Florida and took his first parachute jump to celebrate his eighty-first birthday; he acquired various hotels that he turned into health spas. In California, Macfadden bought the Arrowhead Springs from Conrad Hilton. The night after the deal was made, Johnnie Lee claimed to have followed Macfadden as he shouldered a duffel bag containing a metal box filled with stacks of money, hiked up a hill, and buried it. Another time, he took his wife with him up into the mountains of New York and buried a metal box filled with money, telling her, "Remember the location; this is for you."

Macfadden was jealous of his Johnnie Lee and hired a private detective to follow her, but the detective fell in love with her and wound up shadowing Macfadden and reporting to Johnnie Lee that he was seeing other women. Again, she caught him in bed with a woman.

When they separated, Macfadden's spirit collapsed. He was already besieged by lawsuits over the trust company he had set up to control his publishing enterprises. Johnnie Lee sued him, and his former wife sued him, other women sued him. His fortune dwindled. He spent the last two years of his life in and out of court and in and out of jail. Macfadden lived in a small suite at a hotel in Jersey City and died of jaundice on October 12, 1955. Refusing medical treatment to the end, he had tried to cure himself by fasting.

No sooner was Macfadden in the ground than Johnnie Lee went to the hill above Arrowhead Lake, and looked for the spot where her husband had buried the metal box of money, but she couldn't figure out where to dig.

A few months later, a work crew digging on a rural property that Macfadden used to own in upstate New York came up with a metal box containing $89,000 in cash.

The old crank probably buried dozens of those metal boxes and they're all still there. §

# Wilson Mizner
# (1876–1933)

"He was born with the gift of laughter and a sense that the world was mad."

With that classic line, Rafael Sabatini opened his novel *Scaramouche*. But the author had met Wilson Mizner in London, and the line describes that con-man genius even better than it describes a roguish fictional actor. As does Mizner's own remark to a female con artist: "Darling, you sparkle with larceny."

Mizner was a dozen swashbucklers rolled into one, and his dazzling wit and *bonhomie* fooled most people into believing the tear in his eye was one of laughter.

"If you ever start to tell the story of my life, it will be interrupted by the blowing of a million police whistles," said Mizner at age thirty-five. And he wasn't exaggerating.

He was a singer in a Barbary Coast saloon, a veteran of the short con, a pick-and-axe man in Nevada gold mines, a corner man for professional boxers; he was in and out of jail, lived in Guatemala, ransacked the country for antiques with his brother Addison, ran a couple of professional women, worked as a spieler in Dr. Silas Slocum's medicine show, and roamed the west with a bear he had trained to box. All that between the ages of seventeen and nineteen. He celebrated his twentieth birthday in 1897 by climbing the Chilkoot Pass, bound for the Klondike with Rena Fargo, a Barbary Coast prostitute.

WILSON MIZNER, SECOND FROM LEFT. THE GEORGE GRANTHAM BAIN COLLECTION. COURTESY OF THE LIBRARY OF CONGRESS.

While other men toiled on mining claims, Mizner moiled for gold in the gambling halls of Dawson City. He specialized in poker with a marked deck, until discovering an easier way to get rich. Mizner had himself installed behind the weighing scales at "Arizona" Charlie Meadow's saloon and became adept at surreptitiously spilling gold dust onto the carpet. At the end of every shift, Mizner burned the rug and extracted the gold. He later claimed that this unique smelter process netted him a couple of thousand dollars a week. He only lost the job when Arizona Charlie noticed his carpets kept disappearing.

Once, he put on a mask and, brandishing a revolver, burst into a Dawson City candy store and cried, "Your chocolates or your life!"

Mizner stayed in Dawson City for three years, until the Nome strike, and never did a speck of manual labour in either berg. His best friends were Wyatt Earp and Bat Masterson; otherwise Mizner thought most men in Alaska and the Klondike were "a bunch of ribbon clerks."

In 1903, Mizner left the North for the bright lights. A couple of days after landing in New York City, he began romancing Mary Adelaide Yerkes, who was more than twice his age and married to Charles T. Yerkes, the public-transit tycoon and stock manipulator upon whom Theodore Dreiser modeled the protagonist of his novels *The Titan* and *The Financier*. Yerkes chased young women and paid no attention to his wife's activities, even though her affair with Mizner was the talk of the dailies. "The romance of the Merry Widow and the Candy Kid," one paper called it. Mizner had met her at a horse show where Mrs. Yerkes was sharing a box with Mizner's brother Addison. He spent the night with her and the next morning borrowed ten thousand dollars.

Mr. Yerkes conveniently passed from the scene after a heart attack, and Wilson and Mary got hitched. Had things gone more smoothly, their relationship might be deemed simply "stormy." But Mary was a famous shrew and Mizner was, as a columnist put it, "one of the great rule-breakers of his time." Mary didn't like him training fighters in her Rococo mansion and putting up lamsters and down-on-their-luck con men.

The marriage lasted six months, after which Mizner fled to San Francisco and took an actual job, supervising carts carrying rubble from the great fire. He lasted two weeks, quitting after a newspaper teased him for having steady employment. He was so notorious that even his resignation made the papers. "I hate work," he told a *San Francisco Bulletin* reporter, "like The Lord hates St. Louis."

Back east, he managed the infamous Hotel Rand on 49th Street, home to the underworld. Mizner put up a sign in the lobby: "Guests Must Carry Out Their Own Dead."

Through contacts made at the Rand, he started working transAtlantic passenger ships as a card sharp. Over the next several years, he made a dozen crossings, either playing cards or utilizing his charm and sophistication to steer wealthy suckers to his confederates.

In 1919, Mizner initiated a successful career as a Broadway playwright, or rather, he collaborated successfully with real playwrights. His contribution consisted of sprawling in a chair, smoking opium and conjuring scenes from his past—complete with characters and dialogue—for one amanuensis or another. His first play, with George Bronson Howard, was *The Only Law*. It bombed, because nobody understood what the characters were saying. "A drama critic," Mizner explained after one particularly bad review, "is a person who surprises a playwright by informing him of what he meant."

"If you steal from one author," he told a reporter, "it's plagiarism; if you steal from many, it's research."

After four Broadway plays, Mizner returned to the underworld where, he said, there was a better class of people. Mizner took over the management of Stanley Ketchel, the middleweight champion of the world and one of the best boxers in history. Ketchel was also a champion womanizer. Two days before one important bout, Ketchel went missing, and Mizner finally located him in a hotel room, in bed with three young ladies and an opium pipe. Mizner burst through the door, took in the scene, and began taking off his clothes. "Move over," he said.

Mizner booked Ketchel to fight the heavyweight champion Jack Johnson. So great was Ketchel's reputation and so great was the public's hatred of Johnson, the first black heavyweight, that Mizner was able to make a fortune betting on the inevitable, against his own man. "People don't bet on Goliath," he said.

Mizner sent Ketchel to a farm in Missouri so he could train for another big fight far from the temptations of the fleshpots. When a reporter came to him with news of Ketchel's death, Mizner sent a wire to the funeral home: "Count ten and he'll get up."

In regards to the same incident, he supplied another reporter with a lead that became immortal in old-time journalism circles: "Middleweight champion of the world, Stanley Ketchel, was shot dead today by the husband of the woman with whom he was having breakfast."

Mizner gave a young singing waiter named Groucho Marx his first job outside a restaurant. Mizner had an Irish fighter training out on Coney Island who was homesick for the other side of the pond. Mizner hired Groucho to keep the sentimental fighter company and sing him Irish songs.

Later, Mizner told Groucho he was going to go far in show business but advised him to "be nice to those you meet on your way to the top because you may run into them again on your way down."

And it was Mizner—and not Dorothy Parker—who, at a party, pointed to a woman and said, "If she has any more to drink she'll be under the host."

Mizner was also pals with Irving Berlin, who wanted to make a musical based on Mizner's life. Only recently have some of those songs been released, on a CD called *Unsung Irving Berlin*; they include "Sentimental Guy," "Wise Guy," and "The Mizner Story."

Mizner's flight from New York was precipitated by his bust for running a gambling joint on Long Island. From New York, Mizner headed to Florida to join his brother Addison for his biggest score and biggest bust—it's known to history as the Florida Land Boom. Not only did the Mizner boys make millions selling underwater lots, they created an entire town. Addison designed it and Wilson named it. He gave it a name that in Spanish means "rat's mouth": Boca Raton. Addison used his upper-crust contacts and Guatemalan experience to build pseudo-Spanish colonial piles that Wilson promoted, using the names of such friends as Berlin and Marie Dressler, an actress known as "the Queen of Palm Beach." The heady times lasted for several years, until General T. Coleman Dupont complained about the use of his name. When Wilson responded that Dupont had given permission, the Colonel circulated news about Wilson's shady past.

Mizner moved on to the next boom. That was happening in Hollywood, California; he arrived in town just as pictures were beginning to talk, and no one could talk better than Wilson Mizner. Jack Warner and Gloria Swanson created The Brown Derby restaurant for him, and all Mizner had to do was sit in Booth 50 every night and tell stories. Besides the movie people, he was constantly besieged by rounders on their uppers. Stanley Rose recalled that Mizner showed up every night with a thick roll of bills to hand out. W.C. Fields was a good friend, and he and Mizner spent hours verbally jousting. It is said that Adela Rogers St. Johns would minister to Mizner under the table.

Another female fan was screenwriter and memoirist Anita Loos (*Gentlemen Prefer Blondes*). She had been in love with the Mizner legend since she was a little girl in San Francisco, and her father would bring back tales of the Candy Kid cavorting on the Barbary Coast. When she finally met him, in Booth 50, Loos found Mizner even more fascinating than his legend. "Never," he told her, "try to get rich in the daylight."

Loos worked at MGM and wrote a screenplay called *San Francisco*, modeling the male lead, played by Clark Gable, after Wilson Mizner. Jack Warner concluded Mizner shouldn't throw it away, and hired him to help with the series of gangster movies his studio was launching: "I knew he could provide the sharpest dialogue in the business."

So, much as he had done on Broadway, Mizner sat back, remembered, and provided a line of patter that worked its way into the collective consciousness of North America and the world. Just about everything that Cagney, Raft, Bogart, Edward G. Robinson and Barton MacLane said in the early days of the Golden Age— "You're a mouse studying to be a rat"—had come from the mouth of Wilson Mizner. Cagney once inspected Mizner's misshapen hands and broken knuckles, and asked him how they got that way. "Slugging chumps in the Yukon," Mizner answered. Mizner actually wrote the scripts for a couple of pictures, most notably an early Warner Brothers talkie hit, *One Way Passage*. He described his time in Hollywood as being like "a trip through a sewer in a glass-bottomed boat."

In early 1933, Wilson got a telegram saying Addison was dying. He immediately wired back: "STOP DYING. AM TRYING TO WRITE A COMEDY."

Addison died of a heart attack and Wilson died three months later, of a heart attack while recovering from pneumonia. He cracked wise until the very last moment and, according to reporter Irving S. Cobb, who was at his bedside, went laughing. Or, it would be more precise to say, he died making others laugh. When they rolled in an oxygen tent, Wilson said, "Well, it looks like the main event."

A friend had been unwise enough to bring a priest to the hospital room. Mizner said, "Listen, Padre. You can't be a rascal for forty years and then cop a plea the last minute. God keeps better books than that." He left everything, considerable cash and interests in stage and screenplays, to a woman named Florence Atkinson. None of his friends had ever heard of her. She turned out to be an interior decorator who called him "the best and dearest friend I ever had in all my life." Anita Loos called him "the love of my life," adding that he had "overwhelming sex appeal." It was the type of sex appeal, she said, that one found only "in certain Greek tycoons and aging gangsters."

Wilson Mizner was different from other con men and rapscallions—hell, he was different from everybody—in that he was brilliant and tough, never gave up, never repented, kept smiling, and made you think the tears were those of laughter. He rarely committed a word to paper, yet is probably the most quoted human of his time. "Generations yet to come," H.L. Mencken said, "will be quoting Mizner without ever having heard his name." You've done it. §

# Count Navratillini (1914 – )

He was Count Navratillini and I met him at Niagara Falls on the American side. I was twelve years old and had run away from our new suburban home. He was in his late fifties and, as I later learned, had no home. I had been raised on the streets of a big city and he was an aristocrat, or had been a long time earlier, in another country.

I was trying to figure out how I would make my escape into Canada and freedom but it had nothing to do with the draft; that would come later; it was only 1958. He was about five foot eight, wore lace-up army boots, baggy pants, a sports coat, and a scarf—in August—and carried a cane. He didn't walk so much as he strutted, keeping time with the tip of his cane, *tap, tap, tap-tap*. I burst out laughing, and he regarded me imperiously. "May I inquire as to the object of your mirth?" he asked, his hoity-toity attempt at English made all the more ridiculous by a thick Russian accent.

"You're not the average tourist out to see the Falls."

He glanced about at people on the bridge, honeymooners and families with cameras. "I should certainly hope not!" he said. *Tap, tap.*

I laughed again.

"And where are you bound?"

Hell if I knew but I told him I might head out west to be a cowboy.

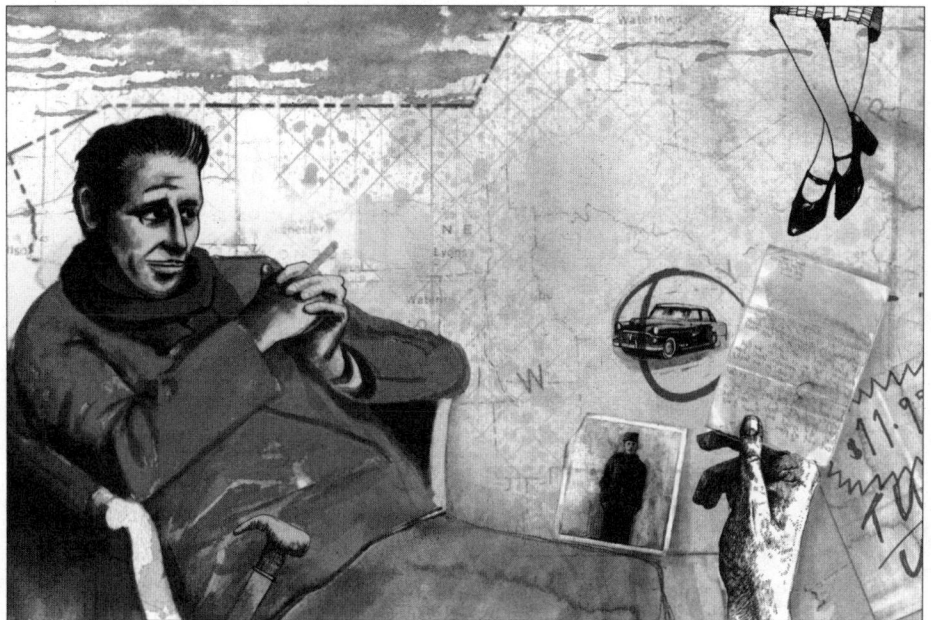

COUNT NAVRATILLINI BY KENN GOODALL. USED WITH PERMISSION.

"Not much of that where I'm going. Cos Cob, Connecticut."

"How you going?"

"Shank's mare."

Since the Falls and the bridge presented an obstacle to my westward passage, I figured I'd walk a ways with him, at least until I could consult a map.

No, he was not gay, a child predator, or a pervert of any kind.

He was an actual Count, born in Russia, and was just a few years old when the 1917 Revolution broke out. His family was able to flee during the confusion of those first months. They traveled all over the world and eventually ended up in Paris. Later that evening, as we were preparing our cardboard pallets that we spread out at the side of a warehouse along the river, he took off his sports jacket and I noticed medals and ribbons pinned to the lining.

"Hey, that's a neat one. The red and gold one," I said. "You get that in a pawn shop?"

"This one?" he answered, fingering the ribbon. "No, I got it in Abyssinia."

Turns out he was a soldier of fortune and military adviser throughout the world for several years. But he had grown sick of it all and now considered himself a pacifist.

He told me that his occupation was walking and looking at things.

"Where do you walk and what do you look at?"

"I have walked most of the way around the world and now I'm doing it again only from a different angle and I look at whatever's in front of me or off to the side."

One thing the Count looked at was women. He didn't look at women all leering and googly-eyed, nor did he whistle at them or make dumb comments. "Quite unusual to see a stylish woman in these little burgs," he'd say, pointing. Other times, he lamented the American diet and the thick legs and swollen ankles that it produced.

"Have you noticed how rare it is to see a well-turned leg and a trim ankle?"

I hadn't, but nodded as if I knew what he was talking about.

"Nothing like a dame with nice gams," I said.

He wanted to know about "gams." Whenever I divested myself of a bit of slang, he'd ask me all about the word and its origin. He schooled me about the big wide world and I talked street talk to him. Sometimes we had unintentionally funny conversations, like the time we were passing through one of those upper New York State towns and I exclaimed, "Look at that sharp Corvette!"

"What? Where?" He looked all around. "There's no water hereabouts."

He was always picking up paper with writing on it, and I got into the habit of helping him out. Once I gave him a flyer from a gas station. He studied it with a furrowed brow. "Tell me, Jimmy," he asked. "Is $11.95 a fair price for a tune-up?"

He pronounced it "tun-neigh-up."

"Yes, it is, Count. Uh, say, do you know what a tun-neigh-up is?"

"No."

One morning he found a couple of rubber toy soldiers, three inches high. He put them in his pocket and took them out several times that day to look them over. That evening he left them in a diner on top of the stainless steel napkin holder after staging a shootout among the salt and pepper shakers and the ketchup bottle.

We were at a shopping centre one afternoon, around back looking in the trash bins. The Count had money—he got cheques from different countries—so he didn't need to hunt for clothes or somebody's leftover lunch. This particular day he found a book of cloth samples. We sat on one of the parking dividers while he gave these samples his undivided attention. I drank a take-out coffee and watched him.

"Count, you're a strange man."

"Compared to whom?"

I got up and walked around and found a paperback book on the asphalt and brought it back to him. He was done with the cloth samples. "I don't guess you'll want this Count because it ends in the middle of a sentence on page one hundred and twenty-three."

"No, no. Quite all right. That's the way life is, you know. It rarely has a tidy ending. It ends, you might say, in the middle of a sentence on page one hundred and twenty-three. For all of us."

The Count read the book as we walked. After we'd gone a mile or so, I pointed to a diner across the road and the Count nodded. It was kind of rundown looking but we were both hungry. The place was operated by a bottle blonde in her fifties who, the Count assured me, wasn't bad looking and still had her figure, which I could see for myself. Right away she had eyes for the Count, and he looked back. When she brought our meals to the table, the Count asked her to join us. She gave legs to his coffee and she offered me a dollop also. The woman fed the jukebox and the two of them got up to dance. I stared with amazement as Count Navratillini moved around to Jerry Lee Lewis's "High School Confidential," and when he shook, the medals clinked and jangled inside his jacket.

The upshot of it was that the Count went off with the woman to her cottage in back of the diner, and I stayed at the vinyl banquet booth that night with slugs for the jukebox and all the coffee or soda I could drink, as well as the remains of the bottle of whisky.

We hit the road early the next morning. The Count appeared happy. "A fine woman in her way," was all he said. Later, he asked me: "What means this 'All the cats are at the high school rocking'?"

The Count wanted to know if I read books and when I answered that I did not, he looked stricken and told me I must begin to read immediately. I had to promise him I would do so. In Albion, New York, as we were leaving the post office, he nabbed an envelope from the sidewalk and repaired to a bench to read the letter that was inside. It was to a local girl from her friend who had gone off to college. The Count provided the details and an entire scenario about the two girls. He said that it seemed a gap had appeared between them, never to be bridged.

In some other town we visited a fat Russian acquaintance of his, who dealt in prints and rare maps. This was an oily character who lectured the Count about bringing a kid to his house. One Russian in the neighbourhood was trouble enough, but another one, an eccentric with a twelve-year old boy in tow, was too much. The neighbours already suspected him of sending reports back to Moscow. The Count just nodded.

They brought out the vodka, and the fat man told me stories of what a rascal the Count had been in his heyday. He had gotten in trouble in some country, Albania perhaps, because the woman he was involved with happened to be the mistress of a government bigwig. There were other stories: the Count in his Foreign Legion uniform at a ball in Paris, the Count teaching ballroom dancing in Guatemala City, the Count and his ill-fated pickle factory outside Warsaw. "*Pickle factory!*" I exclaimed. The Count looked at me and shrugged.

The fat man had a 1949 Desoto four-door sedan and agreed to drive the Count to Cos Cob, Connecticut, where he was to live on the property of another aristocrat of the old school—a woman—and serve as her gardener. "At least, gardener is what he is supposed to be," said the fat man.

The man had to be coerced, the next morning, into letting me go with them as far as the north-south highway. When we got to the turn-off, the Count produced a large photograph from one of his pockets. It was folded into fours and opened to a twelve by eighteen inch version of the younger Count in Foreign Legion dress uniform, chest festooned with what they used to call fruit salad. He looked like Ronald Coleman with a twinkle in his eye. While the fat man impatiently drummed his fingers on the steering wheel, the Count signed the photograph, wished me the best and made me again promise to read books.

I watched the Desoto drive off and it seemed to dip on the fat man's side. The Count leaned out the window and twisted around to wave, reminding me of Charlie Chaplin.

I went to Philadelphia where the cops nabbed me sleeping on a bench at Independence Hall, and called my parents who dragged me back to suburbia.

I kept my promise about reading books and several years later, I even began to pick up letters from the street. I continued to do this until people stopped writing letters.

I never saw or heard from Count Navratillini again. I kept the signed photograph for twenty years, until someone stole it from the wall of my room in Toronto. §

# Alice Prin AKA Kiki of Montparnasse (1901–1953)

There are, one supposes, people who will dispute a declaration that the greatest era in the history of art and culture unfolded in Paris over the first three decades of the 20th century. They may cite three decades in Athens a couple of thousand years ago, or a period in Renaissance Florence or the time African bushmen first began to work obsidian, whenever that was. They will, however, be wrong, and it is not even worth showing them why they are wrong.

In Paris, from the end of La Belle Epoque to the beginning of the Great Depression, everything that had to do with the arts was invented or reinvented. Painting, sculpture, photography, poetry, prose, and, perhaps more importantly, life itself, was reinterpreted. Everything that could be imagined became possible.

The era is remembered with awe; everyone and everything seemed to have a glow about it. It exists in the collective consciousness, like a great movie with an entire city of extras, thousands of bit players and a hundred stars; among the latter: Picasso, Modigliani, Apollinaire, Cocteau, Man Ray, Tristan Tzara, Andre Breton, Eric Satie, Gertrude Stein, and Ernest Hemingway. But none of those could carry the movie; they have their bits, great as their bits were and are, but there is only one person whose name deserves to go

"KIKI DE MONTPARNASSE" BY MOISE KISLING, 1927.

above the credits, and it was a woman, Alice Prin, who was better known by her alias: Kiki.

Kiki of Montparnasse.

She was the archetypal *gamine,* a Parisian street urchin, tough-talking, tough-acting, fun-loving, and available if a guy played his cards right. From the beginning, around 1918, she made a sensation as a model, posing for and sleeping with scores of unknowns, only some of whom would stay that way. Kiki was popular with the painters for another reason; it was she who solved the problem of lines and creases left in the skin from lingerie, particularly brassieres and the elastic waistbands of panties. She arrived in a long coat with nothing on underneath and could get right down to work.

She became a very good painter herself, an actress in art and commercial films, and a popular singer in spots like the Jockey Club and Le Boeuf sur le Toit. She was everywhere. As Hemingway said, "She dominated that era of Montparnasse more than Queen Victoria ever dominated the Victorian era."

But she wasn't from Paris and her name wasn't Kiki. Alice Prin was born in Burgundy and out of wedlock. As soon as that event occurred, her mother "traipsed off to Paris," leaving her with the grandmother. The old lady was used to it; she had three daughters and each had left her with a pair of "love babies." The old woman's place was known as "the house of the six bastards."

It was a mean and tough childhood, brightened only by the existence of her godfather, the local trash man who was also a dedicated tippler. He let her play at the trash dump and accompany him to the bars where she was permitted to drink the remains from the bottoms of glasses left on tables. When the godfather was ready to leave, little Alice would get up on a table to sing and dance, after which she passed the hat around.

Twelve-year-old Alice was scared when her mother summoned her to Paris, but stepping off the train, she knew everything would be all right. "The truth is," she later wrote in a series of newspaper articles about her life, "I had a figure that you'd have a hard time passing up anywhere."

Her mother took her out of school the next year and put her to work. This was also the year that the girl discovered masturbation. "A little nursemaid upon a bench was letting somebody kiss her." That made her feel "funny," and she spent the good part of that day in private.

Alice was a bottle washer, shoe repairer, painter's helper, flower seller, newspaper hawker, and supplemented her income by showing her breasts. It seems they were, as the painters later said, "perfect breasts." She sold the newspaper for five sous, and, for double the price, she'd unbutton her blouse. Touching was extra. "They didn't have to beg me to do it," she said. On occasion, but only when times were tougher than usual, she sold more than a look or a touch.

Her fortunes began to change when she got involved with her first painters. At first, she was a sort of live-in model, spending a week in this studio, a week in that. Word about her got around and she graduated to another level. The first of her great painters was Chaim Soutine, who sang in Yiddish while he painted; the next was Maurice Utrillo, who drank when he painted, and the rest of the time, too. She modeled for Foujita (it's absurd to give the first names of many of these people) who gave her a commission on the paintings she posed for.

Kisling she met in the Rotonde, where they had an argument. An observer described her that evening as wearing a man's coat, a thread-bare cape and shoes that were too big for her. "She had a particular kind of beauty, a mixture of vulgarity, vivacity, and a verbal audacity that was echoed in her gestures, her bearing, her smiles."

Kisling wanted to know who "the new whore" was, and Kiki lambasted him severely. Kisling then did something that was unheard of; he hired her to pose exclusively for him for three months.

How did she get the name? What does it mean, Kiki? There has been all manner of speculation about this. From the conventional—childhood mispronunciation of something or other—to the absurd—a declination of an endearment in ancient Greek. Actually, "kiki" is old Parisian street argot denoting a vagina that is especially appealing and enthusiastic.

She met the American photographer Man Ray in a bistro after a waiter refused her service for not wearing a hat. Kiki knocked the waiter over the head with a seltzer bottle, then took off her shoes and climbed up on a table. She lifted her skirts, revealing no undergarments, and called out, "No hat, no shoes, no knickers, no service."

Man Ray would photograph her famously and cast her in his silent films. Their stormy and violent affair lasted off and on from 1922 to 1928. One time she left him to go to America with a journalist from the St. Louis Post Dispatch. Upon her return, Kiki took up with the Russian silent film star, Ivan Mosjoukine. Being the extremely jealous type, Man Ray was with the wrong woman.

In 1929, Man Ray took up with Lee Miller, but Kiki had already gotten together with Henri Broca, a publisher and illustrator. It was Broca who encouraged her as a painter. Meanwhile, Kiki was appearing in films such as Léger's *Ballet Mécanique* and commercially successful movies, such as Anton Litvak's *Cette Vieille Canaille* and *Galerie des Monstres* by Jaque Catelain.

But perhaps her greatest success was at the Jockey Club that offered jazz, stage acts, and a kind of criminal-bohemian mix that is unthinkable today. Kiki usually went on after the dwarf juggler and the transvestite stripper to sing her dirty songs, many written for her by the greatest of all surrealist poets, Robert Desnos.

But the times changed. There was a Depression. Many of the painters and poets became Communists—the good times would have to wait until after the revolution. Henri Broca went insane and died in an asylum in 1935. Many of her painters got rich and famous and didn't need her any more. At the end of the decade, she hooked up with a tax collector named Andre Laroque who played piano and accordion in cabarets to supplement his income. They became a duo in the clubs and Right Bank music halls, and he provided a home for her until she died.

Men bought her drinks because she used to be Kiki, but they wouldn't stand her a meal and most refused to sleep with her when she offered. Kiki became acquainted with drugs. She collapsed and died on March 23, 1953 from complications due to drug and alcohol use.

Laroque was waiting for her at home. A few days later he told *Life* magazine, "We laughed, mon dieu, how we laughed." §

# Louis De Rougement (1847–1921)

In 1898, a darkly tanned fifty-one-year-old man with long white hair walked into the offices of *World Wide* magazine in London and started telling a fantastic tale of adventure. His story featured pearl-diving expeditions, shipwrecks, cannibalism, native wives, alligator attacks, white princesses, faithful dogs, and bloodthirsty killers. The magazine editors were astounded; they'd never heard the like. They serialized the man's story and soon he was the sensation of the town. The book that followed, *The Adventures of Louis De Rougemont—As Told by Himself,* was a bestseller.

And quite a book it is, from the very first page when the lad's mother gives him 7,000 francs and kicks him out of the house to go and see the world; it's an all-out adventure yarn. Of course, an ill-fated love affair was behind it all. Before long, the young man, having wandered from Cairo to Singapore, meets a crusty old sea captain who convinces him to put his money toward an expedition to the pearling grounds somewhere off the Dutch archipelago. Everything goes well for months but the captain gets greedy and ignores the approaching cyclone season. He and the Malay divers become lost at sea in small boats. Meanwhile, Louis and the captain's dog, Bruno, are the only living creatures left on board the ship, a ship that Louis doesn't know how to sail. But he manages to drift for months before going aground on an island one hundred yards long and forty yards

178 | SCALAWAGS

FRENCHMAN LOUIS DE ROUGEMONT RIDES HIS TURTLE ACROSS A RIVER, 1906. © HULTON-DEUTSCH COLLECTION/CORBIS. USED WITH PERMISSION.

wide. It had one tree. Louis spent weeks ferrying supplies from the ship to the island, just like Robinson Crusoe or Alexander Selkirk before him. Louis was there alone nearly three years before a family of aboriginals washed up on shore. Louis nursed them to health, went off with them to their land six months later. There he married Yamba, "and with her I went through adventures and saw sights more weird and wonderful than anything I had ever read of, even in the wildest extravagances of sensational fiction."

Later, he won two white women in a wrestling match with an enemy chief and . . . well, that's only the beginning. The book ends some thirty years later, with Louis, after walking across the Australian continent for nine months, coming upon a white camp in the outback.

Eventually, he makes his way to Melbourne and over to Auckland, where he catches a ship for London and the magazine offices.

The man's notoriety lasted for a couple of decades, or until he died, but his fame came tumbling down as soon as the doubters got into the act. The first one made himself known in response to the part of the serial in which Louis is with the aboriginal family when it is fired upon by a party of whites. The letter-writer claimed to be an Australian and insisted that white people in Australia wouldn't do that sort of thing. Americans didn't kill Indians either. So this was a case of a liar (or an ignoramus) starting a campaign that purported to expose another man as an impostor. Interestingly enough, the next salvo was fired by a gentleman who insisted that De Rougemont couldn't have possibly ridden on the backs of turtles because the beasts would not allow it. By the time De Rougemont got a chance to prove him wrong, by riding turtles at the Hippodrome in 1906, enough damage had been done.

But it took more than this to bring down the King of the Cannibals; nosy reporters from the *Daily Chronicle* got into the act and discovered that the Great White God was really a former butler from Sydney named Louis Grin. He hadn't been born in Paris, like he claimed, but in Switzerland. After arriving in London as a youth, he began work as a servant. Eventually he became a footman for the actress Fanny Kemble, with whom he toured the world. He had, furthermore, abandoned a wife and several children in Australia. Among those children were two girls named Gladys and Blanche, the names he gave to the white girls he'd won from the cannibal chieftain.

The reporters also discovered that Grin had spent hours in the library of the British museum reading adventure stories. This claim was backed up by a ship's captain and minor diplomat named Charles Milward, who in his journal describes running into De Rougemont in the museum. "I once asked him how he dared to annex an albatross story and make it a pelican story, to which he replied, 'Well you see, zer vas a pelican.' 'But it's not true,' I said. 'No,' he said, his only excuse being: 'But it does come in so very well just zer.'"

It is interesting to note that Milward first went to sea at age twelve, run off by his father, who was tired of whipping him for his constant lies. It is even more interesting to note that Milward and De Rougemont had first met twenty years earlier in Auckland, where the latter predicted, complete with precise details, Milward's own shipwreck.

Travel writing is, of course, filled with lies and hoaxes. There is a whole shelf of books devoted to these extravagances, but the perpetrators of outrageous stories are of two kinds: the outright fabricator, and the exaggerator. Even when the outright liar, the armchair fantasist, manages to write a fascinating book about his supposed adventures, one cannot help but feel cheated over the experience, especially if self-aggrandizement and career advancement seem to be the main goal. The best example of this kind of thing is the works of Carlos Castaneda.

The other kind of writer, the exaggerator, one cannot help but admire, really, especially if the tale has taken precedence over the teller of the tale. Chief among this type of author, in modern times, are Blaise Cendrars and Bruce Chatwin. They had great adventures anyway.

It's in this camp that De Rougemont (I can't call him Grin) should be numbered. Like them, especially Cendrars, he has been vilified, and if you believe his detractors, De Rougemont was just a pathetic loser who never did anything of note but pour out his sorry tale by candlelight in the humblest bedsit. But they use "evidence" merely to justify themselves. It is also reassuring, to me at least, to find the real adventurer still lives despite the attacks, and the real adventurer can be assembled from the facts. To wit: with De Rougemont you have a man born in Switzerland who toured the world working for a famous actress. Somewhere along the line he managed to meet the sea captain Milward in Auckland. Milward quoted him as saying there was no albatross so he used a pelican. In other words, he did have a similar experience to the one he related. It is known that De Rougemont spent years in the United States, yet never wrote about that country. And then there is this piece of information, which the newspaper was able to verify but which it didn't see fit to print since it would weaken their denunciation of De Rougemont: the man really was shipwrecked during a pearling expedition. He survived, alone, on a small island somewhere off Malaysia for three *years*.

Still the tag of "liar" stuck to De Rougemont and he worked with it. He co-wrote a stage show called *The Greatest Liar in the World* and toured the globe with it in the second decade of the 20th century. But things turned bad after that. De Rougemount used the last of his funds to invent and develop a meat substitute that he thought would catch on with the military during the First World War. It didn't. De Rougemont was reduced to wandering the streets and sleeping where he could. He died in 1920, in the West End of London, where he sold matches on street corners.

There's a bit of arcana, a literary footnote, to the De Rougemont affair. The ship's captain Milward, a fabricator as a youth if not thereafter, was a great uncle of the aforementioned fabricator Bruce Chatwin, who was fascinated by stories of his adventurous uncle. Chatwin's early literary hero was that other fabricator Blaise Cendrars. As for De Rougemont, he was a real adventurer of the best kind—the scalawag kind. §

# Harriette Wilson (1786 – 1845)

IMAGE: FROM NYPL, THE CARL H. PFORZHEIMER COLLECTION OF SHELLEY AND HIS CIRCLE. 1825.

Most of us, if we think of England in the nineteenth century, picture dreary life forms in stuffy drawing rooms where lips were stiff and the legs of furniture covered lest anyone get improper ideas. But before Queen Victoria assumed the throne, there was the brief age known as the Regency that followed the late Georgian period, and any acquaintance with the morals of that time makes it easy to understand the reaction known as "Victorian."

In 1793, when the population of London was one million, there were reckoned to be over fifty thousand prostitutes, a figure that doesn't include mistresses or courtesans. Whereas a prostitute got a couple of shillings for an encounter in an alley, a courtesan might receive fifty pounds for an introduction. For sexual favours, she received a house, carriage, cash, and whatever else she wanted. There were popular publications that served as guides to prostitutes and courtesans.

Like most lower-middle-class girls, Harriette Wilson, born Harriette Dubouchet in 1786, could hope for a life as a teacher or a wife, neither of which was a guarantee against poverty. She disliked female company, however, and was easily bored. She was also very attractive, with a good figure and creamy skin. At the age of twelve, her family sent her to a convent in Rouen because "she excited too much interest in the street."

The convent didn't work, and Harriette returned to London and soon became a courtesan, using her mother's maiden name. Given her attributes, she started at the top. At age fourteen, she became the mistress of the Honourable Berkeley Craven, mainly to get away from all the fops and dandies who were after her. She had already been in his bed, and his brother, whom she really wanted, had been in hers. Before she turned fifteen, that brother, William Craven, Seventh Baron and First Earl of the Seventh Creation, had set her up. Harriette discovered, however, that a man's title and wealth was no guarantee against boredom. While living in a house Craven provided, she was being promoted by other noblemen, one of whom, Sir Charles Lamb, "tried with all his heart and soul to convince me that constancy to Lord C. was the greatest nonsense in the world."

Lamb's father was the First Lord of Melbourne, with whom Harriette also had an affair. Next came George William Campbell, Marquis of Lorne. King George III had been his sponsor at his christening. It was Harriette who instigated this relationship, writing Campbell a note promising that if he "would walk up to Duke's Row, Somerset, he would meet a most lovely girl."

He did. They took a short walk and Harriette returned to the home provided by Lamb with a fifty-pound note and a diamond ring.

And so the string continued. After Campbell came Sir Arthur Wellesley, later the country's greatest hero, and otherwise known as the Duke of Wellington. But Harriette soon escaped his clutches. The Duke could subdue Napoleon but not Harriette, who complained, "He groaned over me for hours."

Lord John Ponsonby was next, the only man Harriette admitted to ever loving. His looks were legendary. People swore to the truth of a story about Ponsonby traveling through France at the height of the Revolution. He was captured and hanged from a post but a crowd of women hauled him down, saying that he was too handsome to die. They took turns nursing him back to health. Her affair with Ponsonby lasted for three years. She was twenty-three when he left her, claiming his wife had given him an ultimatum. As it turned out, Ponsonby had taken up with Harriette's fourteen-year-old sister, Amelia.

During this time, Harriette became London's most notorious courtesan. Queues of men formed outside her box at the opera. This box was above that of her sister Amelia, and Harriette benefited from the location by leaning over the railing to spit on her sister's head.

Although she'd had affairs with a dozen men while with Ponsonby, she was avidly seeking a full-time replacement, and candidates were seeking her. She began an on-again-off-again liaison with Henry Brougham, the scientist, barrister, reformer and writer. He had published, at age seventeen, a treatise on the refraction of light in *The Transactions of the Royal Society*. A few years later Brougham founded the *Edinburgh Review*. He was an avid opponent of slavery and proponent of labour reform. It is Brougham who designed the coach that bears his name. He might best be described as a debauched polymath. He and Harriette would be together for nearly twenty years.

Harriette met Lord Granville but told him he wasn't what she was looking for. She soon got with Lord Charles Stewart, former ambassador to Vienna, and the fourteenth Earl of Clanricarde, a nineteen-year-old Irish student at Oxford who was very rich but inexperienced. Somewhere between these was the Third Duke of Leinster whom she would describe as "only about three degrees and a half above a good-tempered Newfoundland dog."

One evening in April 1822, Harriette was driven into the street by the presentiment that something special was waiting for her. She was thirty-six years old and, by her own admission, the bloom was off the rose. There was a new era a'borning in England and at her age, Harriette realized she couldn't help but feel like a relic. Yet she was still a romantic and up for adventure.

In Orchard Street she met a tall dark stranger with a huge moustache dressed all in black. They walked and kissed, but he had to take his leave, which Harriette thought was unusual. They made an appointment to meet the next day at her cottage at Regent's Park.

She had several gentleman callers that day: Lords Boringdon and Clonbrock, as well as the Marquis of Graham, but no one with a tremendous moustache. Three weeks later, the stranger knocked on her door. It wasn't until another month had passed, with more missed appointments, that the man explained he was an inmate in Fleet Prison, and to get to her cottage he had to violate the boundary known as Prison Rules. He was penniless, he told her, imprisoned for debt. He was Colonel William Henry Rochfort. He was allowed out of the prison in order to try and get money to pay his debts. He had recently, as he explained to Harriette, "fought a duel with a noble lord, got a certain lawyer's daughter with child while he was pleading at the Old Bailey, slept with the said Lord's wife, by previous appointment, on the very night after her marriage and … in a fit of despair, proposed marriage to an old woman, backing his proposal with a copy of pathetic verses on her eyebrows."

Rochfort's mother owned estates in Ireland covering thousands of acres but the old lady kept all revenues from her son who subsisted on one scam after another, most of which failed. But he never gave up. A few years earlier Rochfort had fought with General Gregor MacGregor at the attack on Portobello in Panama. MacGregor was the direct descendant of Rob Roy and future King of Poyais, a country that existed only in his mind and promotional brochures. The object was gold. There was none.

Fantasist, romantic, dreamer, dashing, and handsome, he was everything that Harriette Wilson wanted, no matter that he was married and she was being kept by Lord Clanricarde. They were consorts from 1823 until 1831 when Rochfort went to Portugal to help Dom Pedro wrest his brother Dom Miguel from the throne. He came back and fell in love with another woman.

Harriette Wilson might have continued her slow descent in the social ranks and become just another in the catalogue of great courtesans but for the fact that she decided to write her memoirs. Because she had known and made love with virtually every great man of the England of her time, her memoirs, which appeared in serialized form, became a scandal. In fact, they were a scandal before the first excerpt appeared. Not content to just publish and be damned, as the Duke of Wellington remarked she could do, Harriette provided her great men with a chance to buy their way out of her memoirs. She wrote them all letters stating a figure that she would accept for their exclusion. Many did buy their way out, but enough did not; and her memoirs became the publishing event of several consecutive years.

When the money was gone, Harriette resorted to procuring young women for wealthy gentlemen. In 1840, she renounced her sinful ways and converted to the Catholic Chruch.

"I can do nothing and love nothing coldly," she said. "I was created for love, and now all the love that my heart is capable of has turned toward God."

She was confirmed with the name Mary Magdalene.

One of the last things Harriette wrote was a letter to the novelist Edward Bulwer Lytton, which begins with a reminiscence, "When I was a sinner and a *good looking* one . . ." §

# William Seabrook
# (1884–1945)

I thought it might be interesting to find one anecdote to best encapsulate the strange life of William Seabrook. But then his life was so full of incident and he knew so many of the kind of people who are ornaments to any reminiscence that it seemed too daunting a task. I mean, he once walked across Kurdistan and gained weight. Then there was the time he was lost for five months with the Druze militia, the weekend when he and Aleister Crowley, "the Beast," got drunk together in Georgia, the incident where he fell off a Danish freighter after drinking too much aquavit, or that day in Paris when he pretended to torture Lee Miller in a series of photographs for her lover, Man Ray; or I might have picked any of a number of stories from a memoir by his second wife, novelist Marjorie Worthington, called *The Strange World of Willie Seabrook*. He had a cottage built out back of their place in Rhinebeck, New York, to which Seabrook had young women delivered from New York City. "They'd stay in there for days on end," Worthington wrote. "God knows what they were doing."

Strange? Strange ain't in it, as they say.

Then, serendipitously, I came across a story told by Wambly Bald, the Parisian newspaper columnist of the 1930s, and supported by Worthington, about how Willie ate a healthy portion of a Parisian transport worker. Had him prepared this way and that, just so.

But I'll get to that.

THE AMERICAN AUTHOR WILLIAM SEABROOK (1886–1945), CA. 1930.
© HULTON-DEUTSCH COLLECTION/CORBIS. USED WITH PERMISSION.

Seabrook was born in Maryland in 1886. His father was a preacher. His grandfather had been a circuit preacher who rode around on horseback praising the Lord and nipping from the flask that was always present in a pocket of his long coat. Willie went to decent schools, earned a Master's Degree, and got on with a newspaper in Atlanta despite appearing before the publisher all duded up, sporting a cane and a fake beard. He was hired as a cub reporter and promoted to City Editor when, on a slow news day, he jumped out of a balloon wearing a primitive parachute.

He quit the paper, went to Europe to study philosophy, and then quit that to bum around Europe for two years. When war broke out, Seabrook joined the French army as an ambulance driver, hung out with Hemingway and e.e. cummings, and was hit with mustard gas at Verdun.

Returning to the States, he opened an ad agency and gave it up when it started making money. Next, he bought a farm, planted a crop, and walked away from it before anything poked out of the ground. He went to Arabia and produced a book about his adventures. It was the last heady days of an era of exotic reportage by dashing intrepids. With his flaming red hair, his willingness to go anywhere and do anything, and his ability to write like a swashbuckler, Seabrook made out like a bandit.

He wrote books about Africa and Haiti, witchcraft, voodoo and cannibalism, about crossing the Sahara desert and generally just bumming around. One of his books, *White Monk of Timbuctoo*, about a white man who marries a native woman and becomes revered by the local people, is rumoured to be based on his own experiences. Seabrook pursued Islamic studies and became a Sufi. He lived with Zezides and whirling dervishes. He gave the world a bright little plaything of a word that could mean whatever you wanted it to mean: "zombie." He coined the word in his 1929 travel book, *The Magic Island*, which was bought for the movies. "White Zombie" was based on an incident Seabrook wrote about concerning a sugar cane plantation owner who seemed to have had secret power over his robotic workers. The movie starred Bela Lugosi, and not long after it appeared, all North America seemed to have become zombie-crazed. Later Seabrook would claim that he set about on his escapades not out of any sense of adventure so much as out of a desire to run away. He never explained that from which he tried to flee.

There were three things that Seabrook loved above all else: one was drinking, one was tying up, shackling, chaining, or otherwise inhibiting the free movement of women, the third was having them shackle, chain, or inhibit his own movement. Willie dedicated himself to these pursuits wherever he happened to be. As a mere lad, Willie loved to tie up his little female playmates. He said that he loved the desert because the women wore so many bangles and bracelets, and there were all those tent pegs. When he hit Paris, Seabrook became quite popular with the surrealists who made a cult, an intellectual one, of S&M. Here, in their midst, was the real thing; Seabrook was not hesitant to divulge the fantasies that he had realized, while many of the surrealists, Louis Aragon chief among them, seemed to use Seabrook's exploits as their own raw material.

It is interesting to note that Aleister Crowley, "The Beast" himself, was scared of Seabrook. He left several disparaging comments about Seabrook in his notebooks, but this might have something to do with the fact the Willie lent him plenty of money over the years; money which The Beast never paid back.

The photographer Man Ray notes in his memoir the time he looked after Seabrook's apartment for a few hours. His fellow American had been called away for a press interview, and Man Ray and Lee Miller went over to, basically, keep an eye on the young woman Seabrook had left tied to the staircase "in soiled underwear."

They untied her, Man Ray claimed, so that she could have something to eat, and re-tied her before the master got home.

Another story Man Ray told, about being invited to dinner at Seabrook's and being served fricassee à la Parisienne, is probably apocryphal. Man Ray was a guest at a Seabrook party where the host presented a series of tableaux vivants, including a naked woman on a silver platter and others hanging from the ceiling.

In 1933, Seabrook's friends convinced him to commit himself to the Rockland Institute in New York State to undergo a "cure" for alcoholism. Not long after he was admitted, the doctors introduced him to "the pack." He was wrapped one way, then the other, in a series of tight wet sheets. "Tighter than any kid glove," Seabrook would write. He immediately began to get "excited, locally."

After a few nights, the doctors gave up on this treatment, telling Seabrook that he seemed to like it too much. "It occurred to me," Seabrook wrote, completely deadpan, "that I was probably masochistic." His close friends must have gotten a big laugh out of that.

He spent seven months in Rockland, and stayed off the booze for a while after being released but eventually went back to it. There were other institutions, and Seabrook killed himself in one of them in 1947. He was by then the author of a successful new book, his autobiography *No Hiding Place*.

This unusual man to whose wayward character a bit of genius adhered has not been totally forgotten. He shows up in footnotes to books on witchcraft, magic and sado-masochism. William S. Burroughs was a big fan and there is even a gin-based cocktail named after Seabrook and one of his books; it's called a Willie Seabrook Asylum.

Seabrook had a strict moral sense, no doubt inherited from his hellfire-and-brimstone ancestors. Although he might exaggerate some of his stories, Seabrook fretted about doing so. In his book *African Ways*, Seabrook mentions taking part in cannibalism. At the time he thought he was eating human flesh but later, while correcting proofs, realized he had been misled, and that he had dined on ape. He left it in his book and, typically, enjoyed castigating himself as a liar.

At the same time, Seabrook didn't like being a liar, so he used one of his contacts at a hospital in Paris to advise him when a choice young person died. And so it happened, according to Marjorie Worthington, who was there, that Seabrook appeared at a friend's apartment one evening with a pound of flesh from the neck of a newly dead transit worker. He told his friend and her cook that it was goat from Africa. The cook prepared the flesh in various ways: fried, stewed, fricasseed, boiled, all of which Willie Seabrook sampled, taking notes after every bite. §

# Alvin Clarence Thomas
## AKA Titanic Thompson
## (1892–1974)

He was the Renaissance man of rounders, the hustler's da Vinci, only this hillbilly worked more than the Italian. He had no princely patrons, either, but made his money from suckers and fools. Leonardo painted, sketched improbable inventions, and saw into the future. Titanic Thompson created fantastical propositions that reached fruition, and he could see five hands ahead. He made millions at poker, golf, craps, horseshoes, shooting, and all manner of unlikely hustles. He loved women as much as da Vinci detested them. So da Vinci wrote left-handed and backwards? Thompson hustled professional golfers playing right-handed, and losing to them by one stroke merely as a set-up, after which he offered, at good odds, to play them left-handed.

Thompson took up golf when he was thirty years old. On the second round he ever played he beat the club pro. Later, he'd defeat the top players of his day: Byron Nelson, Sam Snead, and Ben Hogan. When asked why he didn't join the professional ranks, Thompson replied, "I don't want to take a cut in pay."

He was even better at poker and at shooting, with pistol or rifle. When an old man and too notorious to hustle, Thompson won the Oklahoma State trap shooting competition four years in a row. He is

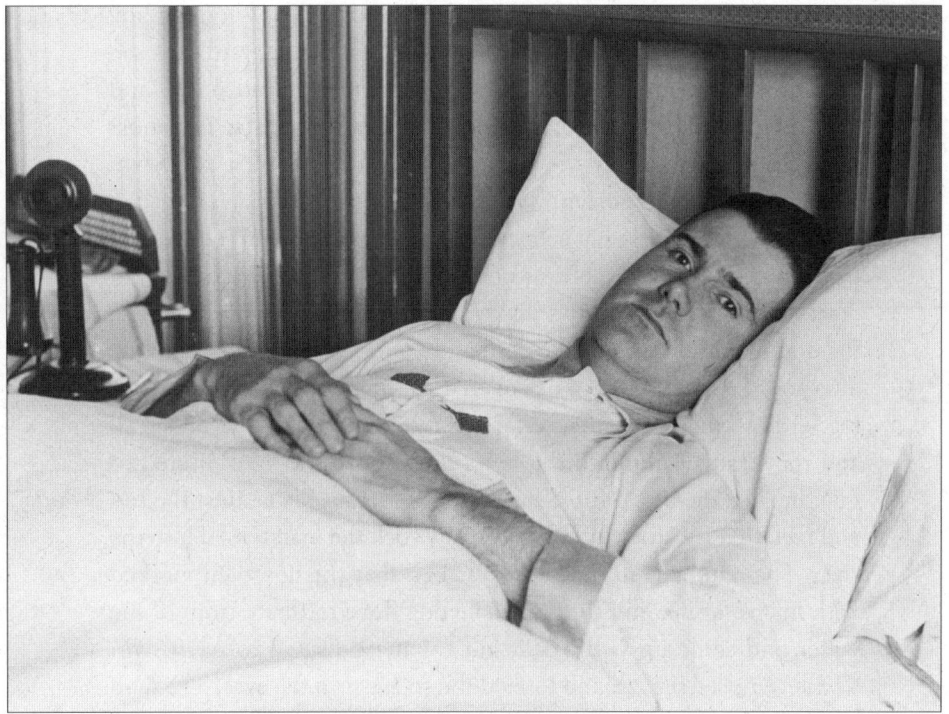

ALVIN C. THOMAS, ALIAS "TITANIC" THOMPSON, IN BED IN A MILWAUKEE HOSPITAL, A PLEURISY PATIENT. PHOTO TAKEN NOVEMBER 12, 1929. © BETTMANN/CORBIS. USED WITH PERMISSION.

on record as having shot five men to death, and there appears to be enough evidence to finger him for one of the great unsolved killings of the early twentieth century.

He was born Alvin Clarence Thomas in 1892 in Monett, Missouri, and raised in the Ozark Mountains. His father preferred gambling to trying to eke out a living on a couple of unyielding acres of dirt, and took off for the bright lights when his son was six months old. The boy moved with his mother and stepfather from one rented farm to another. His childhood was spent so far back in the hills that there was no one to be friends with. When the boy was eight years old his grandfather gave him a rifle, and he soon became an uncanny shot. With his relatives he played poker and checkers, pitched pennies, and threw rocks at targets. For most kids, these were merely the typical pursuits and games; for Alvin Clarence they were portents of his future.

He made his first big score at age fifteen. He'd trained his dog to fetch rocks from the bottom of a nearby stream. The kid would mark them with an "x" and throw them in the middle of the water; the dog would dive to the bottom and come up with the rock. One afternoon, Alvin Clarence discovered a stranger at his stream, fishing with a fancy rod and reel. The boy admired the rod and reel, and the stranger admired the boy's dog. When the man offered to buy the dog, the boy refused but said he'd bet his pet against the rod and reel, that the dog could retrieve any rock the man tossed into the river. The man agreed, picked up a rock that the boy then marked with his penknife, and threw it. The dog dove to the bottom of the water and came up with rock, but the man refused to pay. Alvin Clarence raised his .22 and looked the stranger in the eyes. The man handed over the rod and reel.

The kid saw the possibilities revealed by the incident and soon was on the road, serving a hustler's apprenticeship. Age sixteen and six-foot-two, 210 pounds, he was shooting dice with the owner of the riverboat on which he was a deckhand. The owner was down a thousand dollars, bet the vessel against his debt, and Alvin Clarence was soon the owner of a riverboat. He turned it into a floating gambling hall but lost the boat after shooting two thieves to death. The local sheriff forced him to sign over the title in lieu of going to jail.

He wandered all over the South and Southwest, hustling whatever and whomever. He ran into his own father at a card game in Oklahoma, and fleeced him. He disliked the man so much that he changed his last name to Thompson. It was in a pool hall in Oklahoma that he acquired his nickname. The great new ship, yet to be launched, was all the news. Thompson had just taken the local hustlers for thousands at pool and cards, and someone wondered out loud how the young fellow could beat everyone so easily. Another player remarked, "He's Titanic, unsinkable."

Titanic, or "Ty," as he was usually called, hustled all the time, morning 'til night. When he wasn't actually working he was thinking about it, visualizing cards or thinking up propositions. You'd see him on the porch of a hotel after an all-night poker session or a floating crap game, seemingly at his leisure, eating walnuts from a bag. A fellow would sit next to him and they'd start passing the time of day. Ty, a genial sort, would keep offering the other man walnuts. "I bet I can throw one of these walnuts over the top of that building across the street," Ty would say. "Impossible," the other man would reply. "Wanna bet?" "Sure," said the sucker.

This is a proposition bet. The hustler laid out a proposition, a seemingly impossible one, and greed encouraged the sucker to lay down his money. Ty stepped off the porch and threw the walnut over the roof of the five-storey building across the street. The startled sucker paid up, shaking his head. Ty had his own special walnut with a piece of lead inside. He made over a million dollars on these proposition bets alone.

He hit New York just before the end of the First World War and immediately became a star in the firmament that glittered on the pavement around Lindy's Restaurant on Lower Broadway, an area Damon Runyon dubbed Jacob's Beach. Runyon was so entranced by Ty's tales that he reworked many of them into his own short stories. In the terrible movie made from them, *Guys and Dolls,* Marlon Brando is monumentally miscast as Sky Masterson, who is based on Titanic Thompson.

In the early 1920s, Ty went out to Chicago to confront Nicholas "Nick the Greek" Dandalos. These two supreme hustlers went on the road together, winning millions of dollars all over the United States. In 1928, Ty was back in New York in a game of five-card stud at the Congress apartment building. Among the players was Arnold "Mr. Big" Rothstein, the man who fixed the 1919 World Series, the most notorious gambler of his day, if not the best.

He is Wolfsheim in F. Scott Fitzgerald's *The Great Gatsby*. The police knew him as "The J.P. Morgan of the underworld."

By the time the game ended, which was after thirty hours, Rothstein was in debt to six men—Ty among them—for over half a million dollars. Rothstein gave his markers, but after two weeks when he hadn't honoured them, he was found dead. The police found no evidence to convict any of the men in the game. Recently, however, a screenwriter interested in making a movie about Titanic Thompson has claimed to have proof that Ty was the killer.

Thompson got so much notoriety after the Rothstein killing—not to mention taking "Nick the Greek" for a cool million in a poker game—that his big-time card-hustling days went on the decline. His picture had been in too many papers. When he played cards, it was mainly with small-timers that were after bragging rights. Golf became his new big money maker.

Thompson's high-stakes career on the links lasted a decade, by which time such a legend had developed that it was difficult to get a game. In the 1950s, when he was nearly seventy years old, he went out hustling with a young Lee Elder. The kid would become the first black man to play in the Masters Tournament. They made money as a twosome based on the suckers' notion that a black man and an old man wouldn't be hard to beat.

Byron "Cowboy" Wolford, one of the last of the great road gamblers, opened a card club with Titanic in Tyler, Texas in the late '60s. Even though he was an old man, Thompson was still working propositions on the side. "In Dallas," Wolford recalls, "he noticed that every day at 5 PM, a breeze came up in front of a building downtown, causing quite an updraft. Ty discovered he could pitch a playing card into the air and the wind would carry it to the top of the building. He practiced to the point he could do it perfectly." Ty won thousands of dollars from passersby who'd laugh and bet he couldn't do it.

Not long before he died, Titanic was visited by his first son. The boy had tried to pattern himself after his father, driving fancy cars, squiring gaudy women, taking up poker, golf, and shooting.

He challenged his father, who immediately sat down and took him for sixty thousand dollars at poker. Ty gave the money back, won it again from the young man at skeet shooting, gave it back again, and finally beat his son on the golf course, but let the kid keep the money.

Titanic Thompson died broke in a nursing home in 1974. He'd given all his money away. §

# George Francis Train (1829–1904)

Every now and again someone having read this column approaches with a knowing grin, and says, "You have to be making this stuff up, eh? Or you're certainly exaggerating." The raised eyebrow follows, and the smirk, as if to add: You're not fooling *me*!

Well I'm not making this stuff up nor am I exaggerating. I don't have to. And that's the whole point of the exercise. I feel compelled to mention this now, already sensing more of those upraised eyebrows, given the subject at hand.

He won and lost fortunes, made record-setting trips around the world, hobnobbed with the rich, the famous, and the revolutionary, was an outrageous capitalist often jailed for his radical political views, ran for President of the United States, and was the fellow whom the most well-known abolitionist of the day called "a crack-brain harlequin and semi-lunatic." William Lloyd Garrison may have been right, but that's only part of the story.

How does one approach such a man? Certainly not at the beginning, for his life defied chronology and linear description. Instead, let's start with the beginning of his downfall.

For George Francis Train, that began in 1873 when he came to the aid of feminist Victoria Woodhull and her sister, Tennessee Claflin, who had been arrested for obscenity for revealing the details of Reverend Henry Ward Beecher's adulterous romance with Elizabeth

PHOTOGRAPH BY MATHEW BRADY [TAKEN BETWEEN 1855 AND 1865].
COURTESY OF THE LIBRARY OF CONGRESS.

Tilton, a woman in his congregation. Train had become friends with Woodhull the previous year when they both ran for President of the United States. His connection with the feminist and women's suffrage movements dated back at least as far as 1869, when he worked tirelessly with Susan B. Anthony and Elizabeth Cady Stanton. So, in 1873, Train launched a newspaper he called *The Train Ligne*, in the pages of which he ran sexually explicit quotations from the Old Testament. When arrested for spreading obscenity, Train replied, "Every verse I printed was worse than anything published by these women."

A court case followed during which the prosecution called him insane. Although the judge deemed it not so, the accusation stuck. As a result his vast fortune, which he had earned himself, was seized. Upon his release, and to protest his treatment, Train removed his clothes on the jailhouse steps and strode off naked, carrying an umbrella.

He was born in Boston in 1829 and taken to New Orleans with his parents, who died there four years later during an epidemic of yellow fever. After being raised by his grandparents, Train went to work for a relative who operated ships between Boston and Liverpool, and soon he was running the company from England. After a year in Liverpool, and before he turned twenty-one, Train went into business for himself and headed off to Melbourne, where gold had recently been discovered. There, he was a dynamo of energy with dozens of projects on the go.

Back in America after a couple of years, Train helped develop the Atlantic and Great Western Railroad, then returned to England where, in 1860 and 1861, he installed the first street railways in that country. Soon he was involved with the Union Pacific Railroad as it pushed west across the American prairies. Train was the instigator of two schemes to promote the land along the tracks. He would eventually procure over two thousand lots himself, in towns along the line.

Train spent a lot of time giving speeches to promote his projects, and developed into a fine orator. One observer noted, "He talked on the stump like an embodied Niagara." Soon Train was being hired to lecture on topics of his own choosing. He was a witty and volatile performer who liked to act out conversations, coin phrases, and break into rhyme. He began a speech in Tacoma, Washington by saying, "Seattle, Seattle! Death Rattle, Death Rattle! Tacoma! Tacoma! Aroma! Aroma!" which translates as: Seattle's a dying town whereas Tacoma smells like money because of the lumber mills.

Among Train's favourite subjects were women's suffrage and Fenianism. These interests were later used against him in his trial as proof of his limitless eccentricity. So was his manner of dress. Train favoured white vests, brass buttons and gloves of lavender kid leather, and he waxed his moustaches; obviously he was crazy, said the prosecutor.

In 1868, Train went to Ireland on Union Pacific business and was arrested in Cork for possessing Fenian literature. The local newspaper described him as being "a man of about thirty-eight years of age . . . of prepossessing appearance, with a striking well-cut face and all that vivacity of manner, quick apprehension, and piquant style of conversation which distinguish the better class of Americans."

Train was held a few days and released, only to be arrested again in Dublin, where he served a ten-month prison sentence and filed stories for *Cosmopolitan* magazine back in New York. Upon his release, Train returned to the lecture platform in the United States, working his way west to San Francisco where he sailed for Yokohama on the *Great Republic*, the largest clipper ship ever built. After Yokohama, he kept going. When he reached Marseilles in France, Train threw in with Gustave Paul Cluseret who was trying to set up a commune in his fight against the Third Republic. For his efforts, Train was arrested and spent two weeks in jail. After his release, he made his way back to San Francisco, having completed a trip around the world in eighty days, not counting jail time. As was his custom, Train had sent stories to newspapers and magazines about his travels. Summing up his adventures after his return, Train referred to his trip around the world in eighty days. Two years later appeared Jules Verne's novel of the same name.

Train wasn't bothered by Verne's appropriation of his title and some of his adventures that the author gave to Phineas Fogg; he was too busy running for the presidency of the United States. Although he finished last, Train made money from his campaign, having charged people an admission fee to hear his campaign speeches. The money would come in handy because he was soon in trouble for publishing those verses from the Bible. What money wasn't confiscated, Train signed over to his wife as part of their separation. Again he supported himself on the lecture circuit, and financed another trip around the world. The one in 1890 took seventy-three days. While sailing somewhere in the China Sea, he encountered friends from Australia who threw a fancy dress ball on board. Train showed up in a seersucker suit and explained that he was so dressed in homage to their country's origin as a penal colony. When the Aussies looked at him curiously, he went on to explain that this was the same suit he had worn the previous year while in jail in Boston.

He told the press, "I go round the world every twenty years, to let it know I am still alive." But Train had to give the world another reminder in 1892, because his record time had been recently eclipsed by the journalist Nellie Bly, who made the journey in seventy-two days, six hours, and eleven minutes. Train's new circumnavigation took sixty-seven days, thirteen hours, three minutes, and three seconds. Back in New York in 1893, he settled into a three-dollar-a-night room at the Mills Hotel and spent most of his time ignoring old acquaintances. Should he deign to acknowledge someone from the past, Train might nod but he never would shake hands, unless with himself. He spent many of his afternoons strolling through the streets, and stopping in pet stores to free birds from their cages. He liked to sit in parks, immaculately dressed, ignoring everyone but children. He became a tourist attraction. At night he wrote letters to newspapers protesting labour conditions, the standard of education, and the treatment of children.

Having been plagued with requests to produce an autobiography for decades, Train relented in 1904. He hired a team of stenographers, got in bed, and dictated a version of his life story in thirty-five hours. When he was done, Train closed his eyes and died.

Condensing his life into thirty-five hours is about as possible as fitting it into this column. One cannot even get into such incidental items as the fact that he was once on the editorial board of the local newspaper in Sussex, New Brunswick, where he was fighting injustices inherent in the provincial policy of pauper auctions. Nor can one describe circumstances that led him to be in a jail cell in the Kingdom of Siam, let alone explain how he got the idea for producing postage stamps in perforated sheets, which he did after inventing the eraser-tipped pencil.

Not long before Train died, the same kind of people who had called him insane determined that he had smallpox (he didn't, he had the flu) and used the diagnosis as an excuse to confiscate all his personal possessions and burn his papers. Maybe that was a good thing, for no other reason than it is now impossible to nail him down. Train has been permitted to stroll off into history, naked, carrying his umbrella, and stopping occasionally to shake hands with himself. §

# Alma Werfel (1879–1964)

*The loveliest girl in Vienna*
*Was Alma, the smartest as well.*
*Once you picked her up on your antenna*
*You'd never be free of her spell*
—Tom Lehrer, "Alma," *That Was The Week That Was*

She lived a long, well publicized life. She knew and loved—was married to or had affairs with—some of the most famous men of her time. Now, decades after her death, she is still, if not famous, then legendary. Songs, operas, and movies have been based on her tumultuous life. The most recent film being Bruce Beresford's *Bride of the Wind* in 2001.

All the actresses who have played her, including Sarah Wynter in *Bride of the Wind*, were better looking than she was. One studies the vast photo archive of Alma Schindler Mahler Gropius Werfel and wonders at the source of her appeal. From the time she was a young girl, Alma tended to be heavy, even by the standards of the time. By her early thirties, Alma was thick-hipped and round-faced, her weight and height recorded as five feet three inches, one hundred and forty pounds. Perhaps she was once, as Tom Lehrer put it in his song, "The loveliest girl in Vienna." More likely, Alma wove her spell, and having woven it, everyone believed

ALMA MAHLER-WERFEL, BORN ALMA SCHINDLER; 1879–1964. DAUGHTER OF THE PAINTER EMIL JAKOB SCHINDLER.

she was the loveliest—and if she wasn't, it didn't matter. She had other attributes, and they manifested themselves early on.

Her father was a decent landscape painter whose friends were all accomplished in the arts. Alma studied sculpture and piano from early childhood and read voraciously. At age fifteen she fell in love with critic and theatre director Max Burckhard. The next year the painter Gustav Klimt fell in love with her. He was thirty-five and living with society dressmaker Emilie Flöge, whom he abandoned immediately upon meeting Alma. Klimt followed Alma when she went to Italy on a vacation with her parents, hiding behind potted palms in hotel lobbies, peeking from behind columns in the colonnades. Whenever possible, Alma escaped for liaisons with Klimt in Venetian palaces. Back in Vienna when the novelty wore off, Alma distanced herself from Klimt.

She was next entranced with the composer Alexander von Zemlinsky, who gave her music lessons and fell hopelessly in love. Zemlinksy was the only person recognized by Arnold Schoenberg as a mentor. At his studio, the young girl met people like Schoenberg, Anton von Webern and Alban Berg. No one understood her physical attraction to Zemlinksy, whom Alma herself described as "a hideous gnome. Short, chinless, toothless . . . unwashed."

Meanwhile, Zemlinsky was writing to her: "Your beautiful body: I'm mad to possess you."

The affair with Zemlinsky illustrates two characteristics that would be consistent throughout Alma's life: most of the men she formed lengthy attachments to were physically unattractive, and she criticized them thoroughly while involved with them. She criticized them to their faces, to others, and to her beloved diary.

Men of all ages lined up, literally, at her parents' door. Others contrived to cross her path, begged invitations to luncheons and parties where she might put in an appearance. Offers of marriage arrived as frequently as the bon mots of her stepfather's witty guests. The one she accepted was from the least likely, if most ardent, suitor: the stooped, nervous, unhealthy-looking director of the Vienna Court Opera, Gustav Mahler, who was nineteen years her senior and whose music she did not, and never would, like. They were married in March 1902 and from the beginning it didn't work. Alma had known that it wouldn't. The great man expected his young wife to dedicate her life to facilitating his work. He lived by a rigid schedule to which Alma must be a servant. As well, Mahler forbade her to pursue her own musical interests. He judged her few songs and piano sonatas to be amusing but trite. He was right, which only made matters worse.

By 1904, Alma was twenty-five years old and had two children.

She was restless, and her chores usually precluded any social life that didn't revolve around Mahler, and when he came home he was too tired for socializing. She did, however, have two friends, the composer Hans Pfitzner and pianist Ossip Gabrilowitsch. They visited her when Mahler was on tour or at the Opera. By 1909, Alma was juggling chores for Mahler, which included tending the books and managing their homes, and conducting liaisons in spare moments. She had men visiting her for fifteen minutes at 3 PM on Thursday. One time she was making love in the parlour with Gabrilowitsch while, unbeknownst to either of them, Gustav was in the next room. Mahler waited until the pianist had left to make his presence known.

Then the architect Walter Gropius appeared. He treated Alma as if she was a single woman, calling on her whenever he wished. He had no interest in music and no respect for Gustav Mahler. He wrote Alma love letters that Gustav often got to read first.

Although ill, Mahler accepted an invitation to tour the United States. Not only was the money good, it provided the opportunity to separate Alma from her admirers. Unfortunately, Gustav brought along his physician who was naturally attracted to the young woman.

Alma remained married to Mahler until he died in 1911, after which she enjoyed playing the great man's widow, being guest of honour at festivals and concerts. Meanwhile, she continued her love affairs and took up with the artist Oscar Kokoschka, who was just as volatile and emotionally unpredictable as herself. Their romance lasted on and off for years, no matter whom each one happened to be married to. Kokoschka was her equal and the love of her life. That being the case, it didn't stop her from marrying Gropius.

The marriage barely registered on her romantic chart. They lived together hardly at all. For Alma, it was sort of a novelty: marriage to a man who wasn't considered ugly. When Gropius informed her that he was starting his own school of architecture and design called the Bauhaus, and that this necessitated their moving to Germany, his wife rejected the notion. She had no interest in his ideas and little physical attraction to him; as well, Oscar Kokoschka was in Vienna, as was her new amour, poet Franz Werfel.

Werfel fit all Alma's usual criteria; he was a bit of a genius and not very attractive. She complained about his "Jewishness," just as she had complained about Mahler's. She tried to keep him out of the coffee houses, which were considered low class. Yet they had evidently had a satisfying sex life, and she became pregnant with Werfel's child while married to Gropius, who thought the baby was his. He never learned otherwise and was broken-hearted when the child died young.

As Hitler rose to power, Werfel ignored the threat while his wife flirted with Nazism. She said nothing when the Nazis burned Werfel's books and banned Mahler's music. She began an affair with a priest named Johannes Hollnsteiner, an ardent admirer of the Führer who later quit the church to join the Nazi party. She boasted that she "took" his virginity.

By 1938, the danger to Werfel, and to Alma for being married to him, could no longer be ignored. The couple joined the flow of Jews, liberals, radicals, and "undesirables" circulating throughout Europe, their pockets filled with forged documents. In Marseilles in 1940, they were fortunate to meet Varian Fry, "the American Pimpernel," who was shepherding geniuses out of France, over the border into Spain, and on to Portugal where they could, hopefully, board a ship headed for America. Mahler, Werfel, Fry, his assistant, and Heinrich and Golo Mann, brother and son of Thomas Mann, took the train from Marseille to the Spanish border. Varian had limited each of them to one piece of baggage. Alma showed up with seven heavy suitcases. Alma remained steadfast despite the hero's protests, and Fry bent to her will. She would have expected nothing less of him, or of any other man.

Soon they were in Hollywood, California. Werfel wrote novels and sold them to the movies for lots of money, works like *The Star of the Unborn* and *The Song of Bernadette*.

Werfel died in 1945. Alma refused to attend the service for him, telling a friend, "When they die, I never go."

For a while she revelled in being Werfel's widow. In a few years, his star was eclipsed and she once again became the widow of Gustav Mahler. During these years, the late '40s and early '50s, she was romantically linked to composer Bruno Walter, novelist Erich Maria Remarque, and her house servant.

Alma moved to New York in 1952, having purchased a brownstone on 72$^{nd}$ Street. She hardly left her house in the day, and rarely at night, because she was afraid of black people. She developed diabetes but refused to admit it because she considered it "a Jewish disease." She drank a bottle of cognac a day.

People came to her. She was, after all, a legend. As the end approached, Alma was given to telling her male visitors that she never wore panties. In her last days, she thought she was living in Plankenberg in Austria, and that she had met Crown Prince Rudolf while mountain climbing and was going to have his baby. She would have been pleased to know that her death from pneumonia on December 11, 1964, attracted as much attention as had Gustav's fifty-three years earlier.

Before her passing, a reporter asked her how she had managed to attract so many great men to be her lovers. She replied that she made them feel important, adding that none of them had been all that good in bed, or particularly well-endowed, either.

*Her lovers were many and varied*
*From the day she began her...beguine.*
*There were three famous ones whom she married*
*And God knows how many between.*

—Tom Lehrer, "Alma,"
*That Was The Week That Was*

# Jack Purvis
# (1906-1962)

It was as if the good Lord, or the Big Bang, or just plain chance got confused one morning and crammed a dozen disparate human beings into one corporeal entity. He, or She, or It, set a Dadaist down in the cornfields, a trickster in Kokomo, a nihilist on the bandstand, a jazzbo in the cockpit, a symphonic arranger in the Huntsville Penitentiary. Purvis was, as the phrase went once upon a time in jazz, too much.

    He started out normally, being born like everyone else; in his case at Kokomo, Indiana on the 11th of December, 1906. But it didn't take long for the boy to go astray and get sent straight to reform school. It must have been while in the junior joint that he discovered music, because young Jack came out of there blowing like mad: saxophone, trumpet, trombone, clarinet, and if a piano player was needed, he could do that, too. He attended high school but played in local bands every night of the week. He didn't sleep much—ever—which is not surprising.

    Just out of reform school, he gigged with bands all across Indiana and as far away as Kentucky. Before leaving high school, Purvis toured New England in Bud Rice's band and joined Whitey Kaufman's Original Pennsylvanians. In 1926, he was in New York playing with and arranging for the Hal Kemp Band. While every trumpet player of his colour was trying to play like Bix Biederbecke, Purvis adapted the style of Louis Armstrong, and even cut a record called "Copyin'

IMMIGRATION CARD. JACK PURVIS, 1932. © DUNCAN SCHIEDT. USED WITH PERMISSION.

Louis." The flip side was another original composition entitled "Mental Strain at Dawn."

During these years, Purvis got a pilot's license and into more trouble. Bandmates remember him renting a plane in New York City and flying under the bridges.

In the 1920s and throughout the '30s and '40s, Purvis was famous for disappearing, sometimes walking off the stage in the middle of a gig and showing up weeks or months later in a different city or different country. One early morning, while in Paris with a band led by George Carhart, Purvis burst into the bedroom of saxophonist Spencer Clark, crossed the room and exited via the window. By the time Clark got out of bed for a look, Purvis was two rooftops away. Five minutes later the police broke down the door.

Purvis was back in the States with Hal Kemp in 1930 but left the band when Kemp got an engagement in Coral Gables, Florida, and told Purvis that he was wanted by the police there. That summer, Kemp and some other musicians ran into him in Paris.

Purvis was once hired to back the Boswell Sisters—Connee, Vet and Martha—on a recording session. As Connee recalled, "Jack was uncontrollable—not mean or anything, but crazy." He fell for Martha, the "wild" sister, and she reciprocated.

Martha liked to ride horses so Purvis stole a horse for her, which wasn't easy since they were in Manhattan at the time. He brought the horse to her hotel and when the hotel staff got excited, so did the horse. Mayhem ensued. Purvis did his disappearing act.

A couple of years later, Connee and her husband Harry were driving west to Hollywood where she was to act in a film. Crossing the desert, they stopped at a "diner in the middle of nowhere." A guy brought menus over and said, "Hello Connee, hello Harry."

"It was Jack Purvis," Harry later recalled, "working there. How the hell he got there . . . I'll never know, but that was typical Jack."

It's no surprise that Purvis was enthusiastic about the opposite sex. He was never accused of being a boring date. He usually got what he went after, but not in the case of the harpist with the Fred Waring orchestra, one Verlye Mills. When she'd turned him down a couple of times, Purvis, having spied a beautiful harp in the window of a Chicago department store, broke the window in the middle of the night and carted the harp away. Mills rejected him and the harp. Purvis returned to the store the next night, smashed the new plate glass window, and put back the harp.

He showed up in a burlesque hall orchestra, he fought in a war in South America, he smuggled marijuana from Mexico, he worked as a chef at a hotel in Bali, and he wrote *The Panama Suite*. Sideman Drew Page, in his autobiography *Drew's Blues*, reports that Purvis "liv[ed] in a tree on an island in the Pacific."

One time, Purvis and saxophonist Charlie Barnet were driving through Texas looking for work. Barnet recalled Purvis telling him how "he smuggled guns and ammunition across the border by plane to the Mexican revolutionaries," adding that "he was a big man in Juarez."

The two musicians crossed the border where, sure enough, everyone seemed to know Purvis, who sat in with the local band and by Barnet's account, "stunned all the musicians." But they had to flee because "uniformed guys" came in. "They were talking excitedly, gesticulating and pointing at Jack." Purvis grabbed Barnet and they split, Purvis saying that the guys were "from the wrong side." The men got separated and didn't see each other again for months, by which time Barnet had his own band and hired Purvis to play trumpet. During a gig in New Orleans, Purvis talked his way into appearing with the Symphony Orchestra, performing "The Carnival of Venice."

Purvis was arrested in Miami on charges of indecency connected with his School of Greek Dancing, the curriculum of which evidently consisted of scantily clad women whirling around while he played various musical instruments. He stayed in Los Angeles for a time, arranging for the Warner Brothers Studio orchestra. While there, he became friends with singer and composer Bonnie Lake, sister of actress Ann Sothern. Lake told a story about how Jack was arrested after parking his car in the middle of a tunnel through the mountains, getting out, and playing his trumpet. He told the police that he did it because he dug the acoustics.

In June 1937, Purvis was arrested in Mexico and handed over to El Paso police, who wanted him on a robbery charge. He was sentenced to five years at the Huntsville Penitentiary. While there, he led the prison band and had a regular show on WBAP called Thirty Minutes Behind the Walls, and wrote the theme song "Twilight and You." He also played trumpet in the prison jazz band, and piano in the country and western group. He was let out in 1940 but immediately broke parole, saying that he missed the band.

He wasn't released until 1947, after which time his whereabouts are even more difficult to trace. There is a photograph of him in an Army uniform with sergeant's stripes. It's not certain that he was ever in the army but Purvis probably did serve with the merchant marine during the war. Alto sax player Boyce Brown claimed that Purvis was playing trumpet at the Brass Rail in Chicago in 1952. Old bandmate Spencer Clark saw Purvis in Baltimore in the middle '50s.

On March 30, 1962, an old man died in a San Francisco rooming house, supposedly of suicide. A paper in his wallet indicated his name to be Jack Purvis. The landlord found the man on the floor when he came around to collect the rent. The gas was turned on, but an autopsy revealed there was no gas in the man's lungs. The cause of death was listed as cirrhosis of the liver. Now, old friends of Purvis knew that he used to make a great fuss about committing suicide, loudly preparing the scene and laughing if his friends became visibly worried. The question is, how could this "old man"—Purvis would have been fifty-six—if he wanted to pretend to commit suicide, have known exactly the moment he would die of cirrhosis of the liver and just before that exact moment turn on the gas? And if he knew his death was imminent, why fake suicide? Neither the landlord nor other tenants had smelled any gas.

Perhaps the man was a friend of Purvis's who was dying. Perhaps Purvis exchanged wallets with him and turned on the gas as he was leaving, maybe via the window?

There were more sightings of Purvis during the '60s, the most noteworthy of them being by trumpet player Jim Goodwin who is said to have met a man calling himself Jack Purvis in San Francisco while he was working a gig in 1968.

Intrigued by the story, I decided to track down Goodwin. I heard that he had been playing in Portland, Oregon. What's particularly interesting is that a director of the Jazz Society in Portland told me that she had Goodwin's old telephone number but that she was afraid he had died just three months earlier. I took the number, called, and thankfully Jim Goodwin answered.

I started out by mentioning that he was supposed to be dead. Goodwin laughed, and recalled playing with Eddie Condon, who carried around his own obituary notices from newspapers. Then he told me about Purvis.

"I was playing at Pier 23 in San Francisco and these two cats came in who looked to be in their late fifties, early sixties, dressed like you might expect musicians from the '40s to dress. Slacks, Hawaiian shirts, hair slicked back. Between sets, one of them came up to me, pointed to my axe and said 'I used to play one of those.'"

The man told Goodwin that his name was Jack Purvis. "I had never heard of him. He said he had played with some big deal bands but didn't drop names or brag in anyway." They didn't talk much but the man came back alone the next week, and reintroduced himself. "He was husky, tanned, a healthy-looking guy." Goodwin could tell by the way the man talked about music that he was a musician. "After I saw him the second time, I told a friend of mine, a record collector, and he got very excited. Told me all about Purvis and showed me a photograph of him. It was definitely the man I met."

Goodwin didn't try to convince me of anything, just told the tale.

Whichever story is true, it is certainly more fitting that Jack Purvis walked out of a jazz club and was never seen again. At least, that's the story I want to believe. §

# Index

Algonquin Hotel 17
Allais, Alphonse 73
Anthony, Susan B. 200
Antoinette, Marie 47, 148
Argyll, 6th Duke of (George William Campbell) 183
Armstrong, Louis 210
Atatürk, Mustafa Kemal 97
Atkinson, Florence 165
Australia 67, 146, 178-179, 202
Autry, Gene 30

Babb, Sanora 114
Balzac, Honoré de 78
Bankhead, Tallulah 15-19
Barcelona 68
Barkley, James 133
Barnes, Djuna 86, 89 90
Barnes, Pancho (Florence Lowe Barnes) 81-85
Barnet, Charlie 213
Barnum, P.T. 56, 149
Barrymore, John 108-109
Bauer, Max Hermann 122
Beecher, Henry Ward 198
Bellow, Saul 60
Bellows, George 107
Benton, Thomas Hart 107
Berard, Roxanne 135
Beresford, Bruce 204
Berg, Alban 206
Bergen, Edgar 81

Bergman, Ingrid 49
Berkman, Alexander 108
Berlin 67, 89, 120, 123, 145, 163
Berlin, Irving 163
Bessborough, 4th Earl of (John William Ponsonby) 183-184
Blakey, Art 95
Blavatsky, Helena 124
Blondin, Roger 133
Bly, Nellie 202
Bo Yibo 102
Bogart, Humphrey 164
Bonaparte, Napoleon 48, 74, 148-149, 183
Boswell, Connee 212
Boswell, Martha 212
Boswell, Vet 212
Brando, Marlon 19, 195
Brel, Jacques 73
Bridger, Jim 135
Brinkley, John Romulus 26-30
Broca, Henri 176
Brougham, Henry 184
Brown, Bam 94
Brown, Boyce 214
Bruce, Lenny 42, 71
Buckley, Lord (Richard Myrle Buckley) 38-42, 71
Buntline, Ned (Edward Zane Carroll Judson) 31-37
Buffalo Bill (William Frederick Cody) 33, 36-37, 54, 57

217

Bulwer-Lytton, Edward 186
Burckhard, Max 205
Burroughs, William S. 191
Burton, Sir Richard Francis 12, 80

Cagney, James 164
Capone, Al 40, 94
Capote, Truman 19
Carranza, Venustiano 101
Carson, Kit 135
Casati, Camillo 50
Casati, Marchesa Luisa 49-53
Cash, Johnny 118
Cassavetes, John 95
Castel Sant'Angelo 47
Catherine the Great 12, 46
Cendrars, Blaise 114, 180-181
Chanel, Coco 52
Charles, King of Württemberg 134
Chatwin, Bruce 180-181
Chicago 38-39, 89, 195, 212, 214
China 60, 62-64, 100-103, 123, 202
Chopin, Frédéric 125
Clift, Montgomery 117
Cluseret, Gustave Paul 201
Cobb, Irving S. 164
Cochrane, Thomas 150
Cody, Samuel Franklin (Franklin Samuel Cowdery) 54-59
Cohen, Two-Gun (Morris Cohen *or* Abraham Miaczn) 11, 60-64, 103
Coleman, Ronald 171
Coquelin, Ernest 71
Coward, Noël 18
Cravan, Arthur 65-70
Craven, William 183
Crawford, Joan 17
Crisp, Quentin 52
Cros, Charles 12, 71-75
Crowley, Aleister 10, 187, 190
cummings, e.e. 189

d'Agoult, Marie 144

d'Alvarez, Marguerite 90
D'Annunzio, Gabriel 50
da Vinci, Leonardo 75, 192
David, Jean-Louis 149
Davis, Bette 15
Davis, Lela 57
De Casseres, Benjamin 108
De Rougemont, Louis (Henri Louis Grin) 11, 177-181
de Sade, Marquis 41
de Sainte Germaine, Comte 43
de Waldeck, Jean-Frédéric Maximilien 148-152
Dean, James 42
Decker, John 108
Del Rio, Antonio 150
Delaplane, Stanton 114
Delaunay, Robert 68
Deng Xiaoping 103
Depp, Johnny 113
Desnos, Robert 176
di Cagliostro, Count (Joseph Balsamo) 43-48
Dickens, Charles 134
Dickens, Little Jimmy 30
Dietrich, Marlene 19, 92
Digby, Jane 11, 76-80
Dixon, Douglas Gilbert 89
Dreben, Sam 101
Dreiser, Theodore 161
Dressler, Marie 163
du Hauron, Louis Ducos 73
Dublin 101-102, 150, 201
Duchamp, Marcel 69, 86, 89
Dumas, Alexandre, fils 134
Dumas, Alexandre, père 134
Duncan, Isadora 109
Dupont, Thomas Coleman 163
Duryea, Dan 114

Earhart, Amelia 81, 84
Earp, Wyatt 37, 54, 113, 160
Eckart, Dietrich 123
Edison, Thomas 75
Edwards Air Force Base 84

# INDEX | 219

Elder, Lee 196
Ellenborough, 1st Earl of (Edward Law) 77-78
Endell, August 88
Eugénie, Empress de Montijo 126

Fairbanks, Douglas 108
Fairbanks, Douglas, Jr. 17
Fazenda, Louise 83
Felciana, Lorenza 45-46, 48
Felix, Prince of Schwarzenberg 77-78
Fields, W. C. 108, 163
Fitzgerald, F. Scott 16, 196
Flöge, Emilie 205
Flynn, Errol 18
Foley, Red 30
Forepaugh, Adam 56-57
Foujita, Leonard Tsuguharu 175
Fouquet, Georges 52
Fowler, Gene 109
France, Anatole 108
Franco, Rafael 129
Frick, Henry Clay 108
Fry, Varian 208

Gable, Clark 164
Gabrilowitsch, Ossip 207
Gaillard, Slim (Bulee Gaillard) 92-96
Galliano, John 52
Gandhi, Mahatma 41
Garbo, Greta 81
Garrison, William Lloyd 198
Gaye, Marvin 95
George III, King 183
George VI, King 54, 58
Gillespie, Dizzy 95-96
Goodman, Benny 94
Granz, Norman 95
Greco, Juliette 73
Greck, Nick the (Nicholas Dandalos) 195-196
Grieff, George 41-42
Gropius, Walter 207-208

Grove, Frederick Phillip 88

Hadji-Petros, Cristos 79
Hahn, Emily 60, 63
Hanson, Elizabeth 41
Harrison, George 42
Harrison, Tillson Lever 97-104
Hartmann, Sadakichi 12, 105-109
Hawks, Howard 84
Heenan, John C. 132-133
Hellman, Lillian 17-18
Hemingway, Ernest 172, 174, 189
Henry, O. 112, 114
Hershey, Barbara 81
Hilton, Conrad 157
Hitchcock, Alfred 18
Hitler, Adolf 120, 123-124, 208
Hoffman, Dustin 114
Hogan, Ben 192
Hollnsteiner, Johannes 208
Hollywood 19, 42, 84, 94-95, 108-109, 113-114, 163-164, 208, 212
Holmes, James 78
Howard, George Bronson 162
Hughes, Howard 84
Hugo, Victor 125
Huston, John 156

James, Frank 110
James, Jesse 110
James, Thomas 142
Jarmusch, Jim 113
Jennings, Alfonso Jackson 110-114
Jesus Christ 41, 108
John, Augustus 51-52
Johnson, Jack 68, 162
Jones, Minerva Telitha 28

Kaufman, Philip 81
Kaufman, Whitey 210
Kemp, Hal 210, 212
Kenton, Stan 95
Kerouac, Jack 92, 94, 105
Ketchel, Stanley 162

Kiki of Montparnasse (Alice Prin) 172-176
Kisling, Moise 175
Klimt, Gustav 205-206
Kneass, W.H. 132
Kokoschka, Oscar 207

La Bastille 23, 47
Lake, Stuart 113
Lalique, Rene 52
Lamb, Charles 183
LaRue, Lash (Alfred Larue) 115-119
Lawrence, Gertrude 18
Le Vaillant, François 149
Lee, Maud 57, 59
Léger, Fernand 176
Lehrer, Tom 204, 209
Leigh, Vivien 49
Lincoln, Abraham 36
Lincoln, Trebitsch (Ignacz Trebitsch or Chao Kung) 13, 120-124
Liszt, Franz 108, 144-145
London 22, 49, 52, 57, 60, 95, 122, 128-130, 133-134, 137-138, 144, 150, 159, 177, 179, 181-184
Loos, Anita 164-165
Lopez, Carlos 126
Lopez, Francisco 126, 129
Loren, Sophia 135
Lowell, Amy 105
Loy, Mina 65, 68-70
Ludwig I, King 107, 145
Lugosi, Bela 189
Lynch, Eliza 12, 125-129

Macfadden, Bernarr 10, 153-158
MacGregor, General Gregor 185
Mackenzie, Sir Compton 51
MacLane, Barton 164
Mah Sam 62
Mahler, Gustav 206-209
Mallarme, Stephane 105
Man Ray 51, 172, 175-176, 187, 190
Manet, Édouard 73
Manhattan 17, 36, 42, 86, 133
Mann, Golo 208
Mann, Heinrich 208
Mann, Thomas 208
Mao Tse-tung 11
Maguire, Tom 133
Marinetti, Filippo 51
Marx, Groucho 162
Masterson, Bat 37, 110, 160
McKinney, Johnnie Lee 157
McShann, Jay 96
Meadows, Arizona (Charlie Meadows) 160
Mencken, H.L. 165
Menken, Adah 130-135
Menken, Alexander Isaacs 132
Mexico City 69, 150
Mezrab, Medjuel el 77, 79
Millay, Edna St. Vincent 105
Miller, Lee 176, 187, 190
Milward, Charles 179-181
Mizner, Addison 159, 161, 163-164
Mizner, Wilson 13-15, 159-165
Montez, Lola (Elizabeth Gilbert) 12, 77, 134, 142-147
Mosjoukine, Ivan 176
Münchhausen, Baron 114, 142

Navratillini, Count 166-171
Nelson, Byron 192
New York City 31, 70, 112, 161, 187, 211
Newell, Robert 132
Niagara Falls 133, 166
Novarro, Ramon 81

O'Brian, Patrick 152
O'Day, Anita 38
O'Hara, Maureen 117
Oakley, Annie 54, 57
Ohio State Penitentiary 110

Page, Drew 212

Paris 17, 23, 47, 51, 67, 70-71, 73-74, 78-79, 90, 95, 108, 114, 125, 128-130, 133-134, 145, 148-149, 152, 167, 170, 172, 174-175, 179, 187, 190-191, 211-212
Parker, Charlie 42, 96
Parker, Dorothy 15, 163
Père Lachaise Cemetery 129
Perkins, Florence 156
Pershing, John 101
Pfitzner, Hans 207
Picabia, Francis 68, 86
Poiret, Paul 52
Porter, William Sydney 110, 112
Porterfield, Mary 34
Potocki de Montalk, Count (Geoffrey Wladislas Vaile) 136-141
Potocki, Jan 138
Pound, Ezra 88, 105, 107
Prague 145, 148
Purvis, Jack 210-215

Rancho Oro Verde Fly-Inn Dude Ranch 84
Reade, Charles 130, 134
Remarque, Erich Maria 209
Rexroth, Kenneth 74, 108
Rikers Island 69
Rimbaud, Arthur 73, 108
Robinson, Edward G. 164
Rochfort, William Henry 185
Rogers, Roy 30
Roman, Ruth 135
Rome 45, 47, 51, 88
Roosevelt, Theodore 112
Ross, Jake 56
Rossetti, Dante Gabriel 134
Rothstein, Mr. Big (Arnold Rothstein) 195-196
Runyon, Damon 195
Russell, Rosalind 42

Sabatini, Rafael 159

Sagastume, Vasquez 127
San Francisco 63, 92, 114, 133, 161, 164, 201, 214-215
Sayre, Zelda 16
Schoenberg, Arnold 206
Scott, Hugh Doggett, Jr. 101
Seabrook, William 10, 187-191
Shakespeare, William 41, 133
Shepard, Sam 81, 84
Snead, Sam 192
Soutine, Chaim 175
St. John, Fuzzy (Al St. John) 115
St. Johns, Adela Rogers 163
Stanley, Kim 84
Stanton, Elizabeth Cady 200
Stein, Gertrude 105, 107, 172
Stewart, Charles 184
Stewart, Slam (Leroy Eliot Stewart) 94
Stieglitz, Alfred 107
Stittsworth, William 29
Stroessner, Alfredo 129
Sulllivan, Ed 40, 156
Sun Yat-sen 60, 62, 101, 103
Swanson, Gloria 163
Swinburne, Charles 134
Switzerland 67, 146, 179-180

Tate, Buddy (George Holmes Tate) 96
Taylor, Billy 95
Theotoky, Count Spyridon 79
Thompson, Titanic (Alvin Clarence Thomas) 192-197
Train, George Francis 10-11, 198-203
Trenier, Charles 73
Trotsky, Leon 68
Twain, Mark 130

Utrillo, Maurice 175

Van Dongen, Kees 51
Verlaine, Paul 73, 105, 108, 139
Verne, Jules 201

Vienna 148, 184, 204, 206-207
Villa, Pancho (Francisco Villa) 99, 101
von Freytag-Loringhoven, Elsa 86-91
von Freytag-Loringhoven, Freiherr Leopold 89
von Vennigen, Baron Karl 78
von Webern, Anton 206
von Zemlinsky, Alexander 206

Walter, Bruno 209
Warner, Jack 18, 163-164
Washburn, Charles 126
Wayne, John (Marion Morrison) 85
Wein, George 95
Wellington, Duke of (Arthur Wellesley) 183, 186
Werfel, Alma 204-209
Werfel, Franz 207
Weston, Edward 107
Whitman, Walt 105, 107, 133

Wilde, Oscar 66-67
Williams, Tennessee 15
Williams, William Carlos 86, 89, 90
Williamson, Mary 156
Wilson, Earl 15
Wilson, Harriette 182-186
Winchell, Walter 156
Winters, Jonathan 42
Wolford, Cowboy (Byron Wolford) 196
Woodhull, Victoria 198, 200
Woollcott, Alexander 17
Worthington, Marjorie 187, 191
Wright, Orville 16
Wright, Wilbur 16
Wynter, Sarah 204

Yeager, Chuck 81, 84
Yerkes, Charles T. 161
Yerkes, Mary Adelaide 161

Zenea, Juan Clemente 132

## About the Author

JIM CHRISTY is a writer, visual artist and tireless traveler who performs his poetry with jazz and blues groups. He found the supposedly mythical buried city of Olancho Viejo in the Honduran jungle and has been in the field with the elite government mine-clearing battalion of the Cambodian Army. He has been compared to Indiana Jones by the *Globe and Mail* and the *National Enquirer*. This is his twenty-fourth book.